BEING THE
HOW TO MAKE A
YOUR SMALL

STEPHEN FITZ-SIMON ha
businesses, including the famo
he founded and managed with his wife, Barbara
Hulanicki. He has worked in England and Brazil, and is
currently involved in a number of enterprises, including
a cosmetics company.

Overcoming Common Problems Series

The ABC of Eating
Coping with anorexia, bulimia and
compulsive eating
JOY MELVILLE

Acne
How it's caused and how to cure it
PAUL VAN RIEL

An A–Z of Alternative Medicine
BRENT Q. HAFEN AND KATHRYN J.
FRANDSEN

Arthritis
Is your suffering really necessary?
DR WILLIAM FOX

Birth Over Thirty
SHEILA KITZINGER

Body Language
How to read others' thoughts by their gestures
ALLAN PEASE

Calm Down
How to cope with frustration and anger
DR PAUL HAUCK

Common Childhood Illnesses
DR PATRICIA GILBERT

Complete Public Speaker
GILES BRANDRETH

Coping with Depression and Elation
DR PATRICK McKEON

**Coping Successfully with Your Hyperactive
Child**
DR PAUL CARSON

Curing Arthritis Cookbook
MARGARET HILLS

Curing Arthritis – The Drug-free Way
MARGARET HILLS

Depression
DR PAUL HAUCK

Divorce and Separation
ANGELA WILLANS

The Epilepsy Handbook
SHELAGH McGOVERN

Everything You Need to Know about Adoption
MAGGIE JONES

**Everything You Need to Know about Contact
Lenses**
DR ROBERT YOUNGSON

**Everything You Need to Know about Your
Eyes**
DR ROBERT YOUNGSON

**Everything You Need to Know about the
Pill**
WENDY COOPER AND TOM SMITH

Everything You Need to Know about Shingles
DR ROBERT YOUNGSON

Family First Aid and Emergency Handbook
DR ANDREW STANWAY

Fears and Phobias
What they are and how to overcome them
DR TONY WHITEHEAD

Feverfew
A traditional herbal remedy for migraine and
arthritis
DR STEWART JOHNSON

Fight Your Phobia and Win
DAVID LEWIS

Fit Kit
DAVID LEWIS

Flying Without Fear
TESSA DUCKWORTH AND DAVID
MILLER

Goodbye Backache
DR DAVID IMRIE WITH COLLEEN
DIMSON

Good Publicity Guide
REGINALD PEPLOW

How to Bring Up your Child Successfully
DR PAUL HAUCK

How to Control your Drinking
DRS W. MILLER AND R. MUNOZ

Overcoming Common Problems Series

How to Cope with Stress
DR PETER TYRER

How to Cope with your Child's Allergies
DR PAUL CARSON

How to Cope with your Nerves
DR TONY LAKE

How to Cope with Tinnitus and Hearing Loss
DR ROBERT YOUNGSON

How to Do What You Want to Do
DR PAUL HAUCK

How to Enjoy Your Old Age
DR B. F. SKINNER AND M. E.
VAUGHAN

How to Interview and Be Interviewed
MICHELE BROWN AND
GYLES BRANDRETH

How to Love and be Loved
DR PAUL HAUCK

How to Say No to Alcohol
KEITH McNEILL

How to Sleep Better
DR PETER TYRER

How to Stand up for Yourself
DR PAUL HAUCK

How to Start a Conversation and Make Friends
DON GABOR

How to Stop Feeling Guilty
DR VERNON COLEMAN

How to Stop Smoking
GEORGE TARGET

How to Stop Taking Tranquillisers
DR PETER TYRER

If Your Child is Diabetic
JOANNE ELLIOTT

Jealousy
DR PAUL HAUCK

Learning to Live with Multiple Sclerosis
DR ROBERT POVEY, ROBIN DOWIE
AND GILLIAN PRETT

Living Through Personal Crisis
ANN KAISER STEARNS

Living with Grief
DR TONY LAKE

Living with High Blood Pressure
DR TOM SMITH

Loneliness
DR TONY LAKE

Making Marriage Work
DR PAUL HAUCK

Making the Most of Yourself
GILL COX AND SHEILA DAINOW

Making Relationships Work
CHRISTINE SANDFORD AND WYN
BEARDSLEY

Meeting People is Fun
How to overcome shyness
DR PHYLLIS SHAW

No More Headaches
LILIAN ROWEN

One Parent Families
DIANA DAVENPORT

Overcoming Tension
DR KENNETH HAMBLY

The Parkinson's Disease Handbook
DR RICHARD GODWIN-AUSTEN

Second Wife, Second Best?
Managing your marriage as a second wife
GLYNNIS WALKER

Self-Help for your Arthritis
EDNA PEMBLE

The Sex Atlas
DR ERWIN HAEBERLE

Six Weeks to a Healthy Back
ALEXANDER MELLEBY

Solving your Personal Problems
PETER HONEY

A Step-Parent's Handbook
KATE RAPHAEL

Stress and your Stomach
DR VERNON COLEMAN

Overcoming Common Problems Series

Overcoming Common Problems

BEING THE BOSS –
HOW TO MAKE A SUCCESS OF
YOUR SMALL BUSINESS

Stephen Fitz-Simon

SHELDON PRESS
LONDON

First Published in Great Britain in 1987 by
Sheldon Press, SPCK, Marylebone Road, London NW1 4DU

Copyright © Fiction Factory I

British Library Cataloguing in Publication Data

Fitz-Simon, Stephen
  Being the boss : how to make a success of
your small business. —— (Overcoming common problems).
  1. Small business —— Great Britain ——
Management
  I. Title   II. Series
  658'.022'0941   HD62.7

  ISBN 0–85969–557–3

Filmset by Deltatype, Ellesmere Port, Cheshire
Printed in Great Britain by
Biddles Ltd, Guildford, Surrey

To Barbara & Witold

Contents

Introduction

For millions of us, of all ages, types and sexes, to 'be my own boss' is the ultimate dream. To achieve this goal is a compulsive necessity, even addiction, that drives us forward, planning, scheming and downright day-dreaming of commercial empires and heroic feats of business acumen. The mere fact of being 'The Boss' is the big reward. It assumes a superiority to others, a divine right to riches, the contentment of controlling your own destiny and whatever other fantasies happen to please you. At a stroke you are elevated above your peers, you are on the way.

You are indeed, but where you're going is at best highly uncertain. I have been a Boss, with varying degrees of success, for well over 20 years and I am going to tell you some things which may not give you too many answers, but will hopefully make you aware of some of the questions.

For a start, let's get one thing clear. Any fool can be a Boss, by the same token as anyone can be a brain surgeon or a Prime Minister, as long as nothing goes wrong, and that's the catch. All you need is a sign on the door, and if you really want to go the whole way you can be Chairman and Chief Executive of your own company for the price of a mediocre hot dinner, and as long as you leave it at that you will probably be all right. It will cost you accountants' fees for the annual returns and a few other statutory items, but the potential damage will be limited. However, unless this is strictly a hobby and you are gainfully employed elsewhere, you will not be eating, and this is where the problems start. At some point, irrespective of how much capital you have available, you have to start making money. This applies to everybody, from Accountants, Architects, Barmitzvah Caterers right the way through to Zip-fastener Makers – whatever your chosen field, you have to eat, and I will help you to do this, and maybe much more.

1

Starting Up

Why do you want to do it?

Think hard about this question, and make sure that you have a remarkably good answer. It is not enough that Tom and Dick have made successes and your name happens to be Harry. Tom and Dick may well have acquired a fancy style of living in a very short time, but for how long and at what financial and therefore emotional strain is between themselves and their bank managers.

Obviously there is no set of rules that determine the type of person or business that is likely to succeed, but they do fall into a series of broad categories, in some or all of which you may recognize yourself, and therefore you will gain some knowledge of your own motivation and the direction you should be pointing. Remember that there should, indeed must, be some logic as to why you have chosen a particular type of business, both for your own sake and the credibility of your company. It is no good trying to set up a gardening centre if your horticultural experience is limited to a walk in the park, however keen you may be on the project.

The first and most obvious area for the entrepreneur is in the professions – accountants, lawyers, architects etc. – and the creative fields – graphic design, advertising agencies and allied activities. Here it is very common for a reasonably proficient person, after some fairly successful years working for others, to start up alone or in partnership with people of similar or complementary skills. They frequently begin with one or more good clients, filched from their previous employers, and they are doing something that is accepted by the commercial world in which they operate as a recognized path to the top.

Next we have the expert, either executive or technical, who is an experienced operator in other people's businesses. You are well trained and confident in your knowledge and feel that you can do better without the confines of the commercial structure around you. Although good at your job you may well not be particularly successful in your career. There are several possible reasons for this, the most likely being one of the following.

Perhaps you are so inhibited by the politics of larger companies that your ability to perform is seriously impaired. Long ago I was an executive for an advertising agency. I used to deal with some very big businesses like Hoover, the Royal Air Force and Philip Morris, and I have frequently seen really able people of the middle executive level, responsible for enormous expenditure and who on their own were both creative and articulate, reduced to lumps of incoherent misery in the presence of their superiors. I have also seen complete idiots who knew how to play the game, who twenty years later are sitting there as Captains of Industry, presumably surrounded by like-minded parrots. If you are of the first type, then you are best off on your own. Leave that particular rat race to those that deserve it.

Alternatively you may be so aggressive and bloody–minded that you are a menace to your colleagues. You may be good in your job but, as you progress, your impatience with those around you becomes harder and harder to control, until in moments of duress the veneer cracks and out it all comes. In most businesses this will not do. You will get away with it once or twice and then that will be that. Best get out ahead of the action.

It is not a prerequisite of entrepreneurial progress that you should be totally out of order in the structure of a big company, but I know several people who are undoubtedly of that style who have made very happy and successful lives for themselves by finding something that they are good at, usually something that they could do well with their own hands, and by sticking to it have slowly prospered over the years, and who now, if not million-aires, are very comfortable indeed.

Least likely, but not impossible, is that you have a brilliant idea, an idea of such simplicity, or complexity, that no one has ever thought of it before, or at least in the guise that you are going to present it. This is possibly the truest form of entre-preneur, the genuine punter. You have probably had several such ideas, but always for some good reason they have not come to anything, and then suddenly somethings works and you are set. You probably know little about the business art, and less about production and finance, you almost certainly have little capital, but people are buying your product. Don't worry, as long as you have sales, and some real profit margin, brute force and ignorance can get you a long way. You must react quickly however, because if your idea is that good, someone else will take it up, knock it off, and change it a bit here and there, and all the patents in the world will not protect you once the commercial heavies are on your tail. Make the most of it, but it will not last for ever, so you should be thinking of what you do next while the bonanza is running, and whatever happens you must get off the wave before it breaks. The world is full of hula hoops, clicker balls, roller skates and other fads, because somebody thought they would last another few weeks.

What it is like?

What it is not like is the advertisements, 'Time to go it alone darling' may well be an excuse for a big night out, but it had better not carry through to tomorrow lunchtime. You are on your own, and the faster you can rid yourself of the natural euphoria and get into your stride the less money you are going to lose. From the moment you start out on your own the clock is running, and however far you progress, you will be running against it for the rest of your commercial existence.

Life has suddenly changed for you in several basic ways. They may not become apparent all at once, but here is a cross-section of your altered status.

Loneliness

You are completely on your own. There is no one whose advice you should absolutely trust. Not your professional advisers, your bank manager, your father-in-law or anyone else. However similar you and your circumstances may be to those of others in a comparable situation, you are unique in yourself, and the fact that someone else took a certain course and it worked has nothing to do with your problem. Far better to listen to ideas or methods that did not work so that you can avoid the same mistakes, than assume that those same rules for success will apply again. However genuinely meant may be the advice that you are receiving, you must learn quickly to sift through it and pick out the bits that may be useful to you and reject those that your instinct or experience tell you are wrong in your particular case.

You Pay the Wages

Or conversely, you pay your own wages and there is no cheque coming at the end of the month, unless it is signed by yourself. If you are not in the habit of receiving wages you will not notice much difference, but those of you who are already with families, mortgages and other status symbols are in for a shock. If the money is not there you have a problem – your wife will be miserable, your child's headmaster will change from a smirking flunkey to a threatening nightmare, the building society will start to ask what is going on, and all that you have worked for, and presumably hold in some esteem, will start to drag you down, and distract you from the main task, the survival of the business. The more you have, the more you stand to lose.

Your Personal Credit Rating

If you have never had one, this is not a big worry, but if you are used to a regular salary, you will have built an overdraft with your bank, you may be buying your dwelling, you have the odd credit card, and some hire purchase because you are in regular employment. The moment you are on your own all this starts to change. Whatever you do, tell as few of these credit sources as possible of your new status. Clearly the bank manager has to know, as you have probably, and mistakenly, opened your business account in his branch anyway, but let the rest find out for themselves. Make sure you pay them on time, or they will quickly smell a rat and you will find yourself with another set of problems of a most unpleasant nature.

If you need to apply for HP or lease equipment for your business you may find it very difficult unless you can arrange this under your own name while you are still enjoying a salary. Finance companies work to a very strange set of criteria. You will find that on day one of your company's existence you can give an employee a reference which will enable him to get a loan for a new car, while you as the director will have to show two or three years trading figures for the same company before they will even consider you. In particular, watch the bank. You may have been a favoured client while on a salary, but on your own you are looked upon as a potential liability. The manager, who last week would have given you a loan for an extension to your house in five minutes, now starts to ring you up if you are £50 overdrawn. More advice about this, though, later in the book.

Partners

Whether or not you should have a partner on day one of your enterprise depends very largely on your own drive and egotism. However much you may need the assistance of others, you must make sure that you are the dominant party in the relationship. If not, you are better off forgetting the whole idea and starting something else.

There are only two good reasons for needing a partner or partners at the conception of a business, and these are to provide you with one or other of the following.

(a) *Skill or connection*

If you are, say, a salesman, you may well need a designer, technical expert or production person to provide you with a product for you to sell. Conversely, if you are not a salesman but have a marvellous talent or idea, it is imperative that you are with someone who has the ability and connections to convert your product into orders. Most businesses have these two elements, the creative – designing, buying, copywriting etc. – and the commercial. The more closely these two functions are linked at every level, the greater are your chances of success, so your choice of partner must be based not only on professional skill, but personal compatibility. You are going to see more of your partner than of your husband, wife or paramour, and if things go well, you will be with them for a very long time. This does not mean that you have to be close friends. It means that while at work you must respect one another's abilities and, overall, you must trust each other. I do not mean this in the sense of being ripped off, although I have known this to happen but in the areas of dedication and determination. However good you

7

are you will encounter problems that can, if not properly handled, wipe you out. This is when you will demonstrate your right to be the boss and you will need the unequivocable support of your fellow bosses. A weak partner is more dangerous than a strong enemy, and much harder to eliminate.

(b) *Capital*

This is what it is all about – real money. Not projections, not cash flow but real cash that is there in the bank on day one. We will discuss how much you need and how to get it later on, but assuming that you personally do not have the wherewithal, then one of your first considerations must be to find some other party who has.

Over the years I have been in partnership on several occasions. Some have worked out and others been a nightmare. There are certain basics that you should know.

Commitment

Your partners must have sufficient cash or assets to match your own. More important, they must have the irrevocable commitment to use them. Things can go very wrong at the start of a business. Often more capital is needed than was first thought, and if you are prepared to mortgage your entire life on the success of your idea you must be absolutely sure that your partner(s) feel likewise, and can persuade their families and advisers. They all have to be as dedicated as you are, and this is hard to know until the moment comes when your entire financial life is up for grabs.

A small story here to show what I mean. I thought I was going to make a big business by selling clothes by mail order. I made the mistake of involving someone I knew. I did not ask him for money, and I paid him a top wage and said he could have 25% of the company. In the first six months the company sold above expectations, but for various reasons it lost money. However, all my 'partner' could see was about £20,000 a week being banked, so as far as he was concerned I was a crook. He insisted on his 25%. As you can imagine, I was well pleased with his attitude, but I gave it to him. Comes the end of the week and he rings me up.

'Fitz, we do not have enough money in the bank to pay the wages.'

I say 'Why not?',

'Because we need £1,000 and you only put in £750', or something like that.

So I said, 'But I don't have to put in £1,000 any more. You have 25% so you put in £250 and there is no problem'. End of partnership. He wanted to make the money but he was not prepared to lose it. In fact, he had much more capital than I did, but he could not conceive that he would ever have to put his hand into his own pocket, although he was very happy to put it into mine.

Friends and Relations

As partners these must be avoided at all costs. For a start they will have wants that you cannot afford to grant. These are

(a) Proprietorial rights
(b) A fixed return

Because they have lent you some money, they think that they own the business, *and* they want a fixed return on their investment, irrespective of the ability of the company to pay it. Little Auntie Maud, who has put up her £5,000 and who has been a mouse for the first 65 years of her life, will suddenly turn into a fire-breathing tortoise. She will arrive at your place of work, and in five minutes can destroy your entire image with staff, customers, creditors and whoever else happens to be on hand.

Friends are even worse. I know a man who had a small partnership in a restaurant. As an eating place it was neither good nor bad. He had a fair chef-come-manager and they would probably not have come to too much harm if my friend had not coerced large parties of his own friends to go and eat there. I was in one such a party; the locals were having a nice quiet, intimate evening until our investor arrived. Suddenly Sloane Square has been transported to Battersea. Our friend starts to make his interest known, chairs and tables are shifted, the Cook/Manager is hauled out of the kitchen and made to perform, the regulars who went there to eat start to become depressed and three days later the cook does a bunk with two weeks takings and the company car. He just could not stand it and I cannot blame him.

Sleeping Partners

The idea is great – some entity, individual or consortium, a merchant bank or institution, puts the money in, takes a percentage of the business and goes home to wait for the results of your efforts. As long as everything is going broadly as intended your sleeper will remain dormant, but the minute something goes amiss the relationship changes, particularly if your partner has more financial strength than yourself.

The first question is, what does 'going amiss' mean? Much depends on the terms of your finance. Most non-European investors look to a 3–5 year plan before their money starts to come back. If you are dealing with Japan you may well have over 10 years to prove yourself with a capital structure tailored for this eventuality. In Europe you, the entrepreneur, are usually expected to show at least a break even on day one, which in most types of business simply does not happen. After this the investors start to get restive and your sleeper suddenly becomes exceedingly active. The smaller they are in terms of financial resources the more involved they are determined to be, as if the mere fact that they have money at risk gives them the automatic access to specialized knowledge of your area of activity. You will find that your time and, far worse, your thought processes and self-confidence are being eroded by the need to explain your every move to people who have already adopted the self-righteous attitude of the ill-advised. Yesterday's joint decisions become your personal responsibility; small errors and inconsistencies so trivial that you cannot remember them are produced as damning evidence of your managerial incompetence and overnight your fair-weather partners are by implication accusing you of anything that they can lay their hands on, from grand larceny to fiddling the petty cash. This happens most often if your 'partners' are themselves employees and not the actual owners of the money invested.

This brings us to what is perhaps the best sort of partner. This is a trading company in an allied field. This means people who are already established in a type of business to which your own product or service is both complementary and non-competitive.

If you know what you are doing and have a reasonably fresh

approach to the subject, somewhere out there is an established company that is looking for what you have to offer. If you are lucky enough to come into contact with this situation early in your career as a boss you can do yourself and them a power of good. They can offer money, resources and advice that could take you a lifetime to acquire, and as long as the deal is carefully and legally documented, so that your own position as head of your own cabbage patch is clearly defined and protected, you can go a long way very quickly. The drawback for this sort of arrangement is that your partner will eventually want, and deserve, a large percentage of the equity in your business. This is fine as long as the control of their own business does not change, but things happen fast in the world of money. After five highly profitable years with a retailing partner I read in the evening newspaper that I was now owned by a property company, and that was the beginning of the end for me and my company. The thing I did learn at that time was that, if you do a deal with another boss, everything will be fine as long as you keep your direct contact. Your interests are the same and deep down you are probably thinking the same. It is when you allow the flunkies to get between you that you are on the slippery slope.

However frantic you are for capital at a given moment remember that very few of those who can honestly get back a wad of one million pound notes and say 'These are mine', have ever had a true partner in their lives. They may have stepped in and out of bed with a few people in various moments of crisis, but they themselves have never been partners, they have merely used others to help them along the way – be careful that you are not one of the others.

Capital

There are three types of capital expenditure to be considered at the start of a business. The first is for the purpose of buying the fixed assets absolutely necessary for the operation to function. It is virtually impossible to acquire the use of a worthwhile retail or restaurant premises without the payment of a very substantial premium. Depending on the deal, this can be money very well spent, and with luck your asset will appreciate in the natural movement of the market or by the success that you are yourself enjoying, and can become a source of capital gain or collateral in the future. Not so with factory and office premises. Here the market is far more volatile, and buildings relatively easy to rent, without premium. I can see no advantage in spending valuable capital for such a place, nor indeed for the machinery that goes into it, when with some shopping around you can probably lease the lot, even as a new business. You will still need some money for the down payment but after that the rental payments are directly deductible from taxes, and you are saving your cash for what lies ahead.

Once you have taken premises, you have to decorate them. In a retail/restaurant business the decor and fittings are obviously critical to your success. Even in the strictly industrial environment, your workers will be far more efficient in a clean and bright building than in the breeze-block tips that frequently pass for modern industrial units. Whatever the reason, it is essential that the place of work is properly fitted and decorated to maximize its use. It is also a key part of your corporate image, but remember that money spent on decoration is money gone for ever. No matter how marvellous it looks or how it shows in your balance sheet, it only has value to you as long as you are using it. Only in the very rarest circumstances will it cause your property to appreciate. So think carefully, not only about what you want to do, but how you are going to do it. There is no point in building an ocean liner if all you need is a Hollywood front.

The above two kinds of capital expenditure are straightforward and simple to evaluate. There is a known cost and you can either afford it or not. The third type is another matter entirely. It is your *stock in trade and working capital*. This applies to every sort of business. Even if you are a designer or consultant setting up on your own, your stock in trade is you and your employees, the place where you sit, and your portfolio of samples. This is just as much stock, in so far as it has to be paid for before a sale is made, as are the wares of a shop-keeper. The unknown factors are when sales will be made, how much they will be and when they will be paid for. Other key factors are your direct costs in making a sale, your order delivery cycle and the cost of financing that, and your minimum operating overheads.

There are very few businesses where you can turn your stock or service round so quickly that you receive your payment before you have to pay the cost of your sales. You have to take a pessimistic view. Even if you are starting up with proven good customers, the fact that they have come with you, particularly if you are a service industry, shows a certain footloose quality that can turn against you. Remember, you are the new business, not they, and they will be very aware of their importance to you and may well try and take advantage.

In all non-cashtaking business the real problem is 'when will you be paid?' From your point of view the knowledge of exactly when the cheque will arrive is almost as important as receiving it. If you know that a customer *always* pays 30 days late you can plan your flow of cash accordingly. It is when you have absolutely no idea what to expect that your real troubles begin. There are ways of reducing the extent of this problem, but ultimately cash is the life-blood of business, and if it does not receive regular transfusions it will die.

The situation with shops, where cash is received at the moment of sales is clearly different. You should have a regular and quickly forecastable flow of cash coming through the till, and as long as you are taking enough to cover overheads you should not have too many difficulties with the payments to your staff, your landlord and day-to-day expenses. Do not assume that your takings will be such that they will enable you to pay any significant percentage of the cost of your initial stock. A new business simply has neither the credit or credibility to start messing around with payments to suppliers so initially you will need capital to cover these. To the salesman you may be a valued customer, but to the Accounts Receivable office you are only as good as your money, and to be in a situation where you cannot restock winners because you have not paid for the previous delivery will put you in trouble very quickly indeed.

In a restaurant or newsagency, where the value of stock held is turned over very quickly indeed, the cash problem is relatively simple. As long as you are taking the money, and have reduced your employees' pilfering to an acceptable minimum, you should have a relatively easy ride. In fact, you should not have a cash

13

flow problem at all, but keeping the seats full and stopping the thieving are a life's work in themselves.

So we return to the question of how much you will need. The simple answer is 'as much as you can get'. By going into business on your own you are entering into a high risk occupation where the money, when it comes, is never really yours – it is held in trust by you against the time when things go wrong.

This may seem a glib answer to a very big question, but it is the truth. You will really have no idea, on day one, what your short-term cash needs will be, however much you have researched the market, however many clients you are bringing with you, or firm orders are in your pocket. It is amazing how verbal commitments from people that you have known for years disappear over the horizon once the going gets serious. A friend of mine in Brazil, a very shrewd man, imported a £200,000 machine on the strength of the promises of his friends of 30 years in the synagogue and he never had a single order. It is still sitting there in its original wrappings. It nearly broke him at the time, but he is still operating on a huge scale 15 years later, because he is a true entrepreneur, and he talked and worked his way out of it. However, he had made the 'eggs in one basket' mistake, and he suffered accordingly.

Ways and cautions of raising Capital

Two basic rules:

(a) The more you need, or ask for, the more you are likely to get
(b) Whatever your idea, the capital will be backing you personally and your enthusiasm and ability to perform

Let us look at point (a). If you have a reasonable idea that is going to cost £500,000 or so to set up and shows a reasonable return on the money invested, plus a way for the partners to get their money out at a capital gain in a fairly short period, then you are in with a very good chance of scoring, certainly if the area in which you are operating is popular at the moment. The 'flavour of the month' syndrome is vital at this level of borrowing. If you were starting a 'Silicon Valley' business five years ago you would have had people queuing up to do deals, very much to your advantage, whereas today you could not buy them a lunch because the market has become a disaster. Hundreds of people like you rushed to cash in and all they did was break their teeth on the stone because the fruit was long gone.

If you have a big idea, big in the terms of capital, you must go to big people who have the financial capacity to perform. These are hard to come by and the difference between the genuine article and the rogue is marginal. You will only be able to raise money of this magnitude if you already have a track record of achievement in the field that you are trying to enter. You should have been talking to banks of all types, Clearing, Investment and Venture Capital, and have the whole thing sewn up before you begin to start up. Be careful though, because the world is, unfortunately, very small, and the wrong word in the wrong ear can find you with no job and no investors about two minutes after you have opened your mouth.

Unfortunately, if you are trying to borrow very large sums, the investors will not only be backing you personally. You will have to show a committed management team who are going to start with you before you will be considered. Investors like to know that there are a number of cut-out points between you personally and the money that they are putting up. No one is going to give you a cheque for a million pounds without being very sure that they are not going to get a thank you letter from Costa Rica. So therefore you have a nice problem to resolve.

The number of brilliant advertising agencies that I was going to start with friends who worked with me was one a week, but the friends, many of them now big people in their own right, really never wanted to leave the protection of the corporation. They were Company men and very good at it. They did not want the ultimate responsibility that you crave. Be very careful who you talk to.

Management Buy-Outs On the assumption that your track record or those of your associates is such that you can make a real commercial case for your enterprise you have a number of routes to take in the capital sense.

Popular at the moment both in Europe and the USA is the management buy-out. This is your softest touch. If you are a part

15

of a larger concern that is not doing very well and you can show that as an independent unit you are profitable you have potential for a leverage buy out. This really means blackmail. You are telling the lawful owners of your company that if they do not sell to you, you will leave and start up the whole thing again in direct competition. Also, as you and your team will not co-operate with any other buyer, the value of the business will be much less than the amount that you are offering. If you can get away with this, and can perform reasonably well for the next couple of years, you have your goldmine. Financial institutions will be happy to back you against the capital assets of the company and probably leave you and your co-directors with between 10–15% of the equity. If you then do well, the investors will want to sell and you can cash in, and even if you do badly you still have your shares, and a buyer of the company will have to pay you whatever is the going rate. Either way you have had something for nothing and will make money accordingly, but be sure that you make enough money to set yourself up for life, because no sensible employer will ever want to know you again.

Local Enterprise Schemes If you are not in the happy position of the leverage/blackmail deal, you still have a number of options that can lead to a very well-financed start, particularly, in the UK, if you are able to show that you are going to give employment to others. Many areas have enterprise schemes, which can offer you big incentives including cash to go there. With the end of the Greater London Council it is probably better if you have some knowledge of the business that you are about to start. In GLC days the less you knew and the more different from the norm you were, the better your chances, but those happy times are over and you must take your chance with the rest of us.

Venture Capital Funds These are normally linked to the Government's Business Expansion Scheme, whereby those who have money and a tax liability are able to invest with a large tax deduction, at present 40%, if they do not sell the shares in either the Capital Fund or your company for at least five years. The way the investors can take their money out is by selling their equity, with either a take-over of your company or a public float after the statutory five years. You must therefore be very sure that you are going to be ready for this in the prescribed time, or you could well find that your interests and those of your investors have suddenly parted company, to your detriment. Remember, investors are just that and nothing more. They are not there to bail you out in times of trouble. They have made their money, they want their return.

Investors in Industry This is a form of merchant bank set up by the Big 4 clearing banks and promoted by the government of the day. They do put money into start-up situations, and to date they have had a very high failure rate, mainly caused by their own bureaucratic inability to react to changing circumstances. They will let the ship sink for the proverbial piece of tar, but they are there and have money, ostensibly for you. Good luck.

Private Investors Because of the various tax relief schemes that I have just mentioned, these are becoming rare. The person with cash available is in truth far better off spreading his risk through a recognized fund that does it for him than being involved in an individual situation. This leads us to the last resource for the punter who is looking for a large £500,000 plus investment.

Funny Money The way things work in the British Isles, the only people with this type of cash are bank robbers or criminals from other places. Forget the rich Arab and the man who just sold his company in South Africa and has a suitcase full of Krugerrands. The former was always much more interested in spending than investing, and the latter is probably a crook anyway with a case full of local masonry. In either event the indigenous punter has taken so many of them to the cleaners in the last several years that they are busy being robbed elsewhere, and all we are left with are the carpetbaggers who you definitely do not need.

Of course, there are always the so-called organized criminals who, honourable as they undoubtedly are, tend to have a slightly different attitude from ourselves – men with guns and bodies in ditches are great to read about, as long as you are not involved, but having had a smell of it in Brazil, I prefer to pass. As I get older I simply cannot stand the aggravation. That is my opinion, but the money is always there for a good proposition, if you need it and if you can face it.

Second rule to remember is that the capital you raise will be backing you and your ability to perform. There you are, on your own, with great determination, some skill and no money. Where do you go and what do you have to offer, and what do you really have on your side? Probably more than you think. You are giving yourself, you career, your expectations of success and aspirations for your future, and you are not intending to fail. Whoever you are speaking to – friends, family, banks – you must allow your determination and ambition to show. Do not overdo it, though. 'I will be a millionaire in three years', will not endear you to the masses, nor to your bank, which is another place that you must visit.

Clearing Banks Again some rules here.

(a) Do not go to the bank that has your domestic, and probably your only, account. Banks are there to attract customers as much as you are, and a new account will be looked on with a more favourable eye from a new manager than one who has known your puny overdraft and your struggles to keep within it for the last 10 years.

(b) Find someone who you know is of good financial standing to introduce you to their bank. If you have an accountant who has some clients with money concentrated in one bank, which is often the case, get him to introduce you there, or likewise your solicitor.

Unhappily the tendency in all banks today is to reduce the loan-making parameters of the local branch manager. You are rarely talking to the person who will make the decision. Some years ago, you would have been speaking to a man who could give you a £20,000 overdraft on the spot – no security, just on his say-so. Today the average manager has virtually no say at all, and you will never get to meet the person who turns you down. In reality too many fancy propositions have been made to too many gullible managers by people like you and me, and so this element has been reduced, and only the figures count, which if you are starting up in a small way, will not look too good.

What makes the difference is collateral. What can you scratch up? Do you have a house, and more important, if you do, do your wife, live-in lover, and any offspring, want you to risk losing it? If they do not, either get rid of them, or scrap the enterprise. Your bank will wish you to put everything that you have behind your venture, and this is why I have said never use your personal bank for your initial overdraft. Try and keep your personal wealth, or lack of it, a mystery and ride on the backs of others.

Most bank managers can give you up to £10,000 at their own discretion, and some of the old-timers can give you two or three times this, so seek them out. Don't waste your time on old managers in small banks, or young ones either. They are either time-servers or incompetents and their bosses will know this. All they want is a clean nose, and you, being a risk, are exactly the person who is going to pay for lunch and have nothing in return, except a long-winded letter explaining the current policy on your type of proposition – no go.

Finally we come down to what, ostensibly, is the worst case. You have no savings, no assets and maybe no fixed abode. The fact that you are reading this book, even though you might have nicked it, means that at least you are alive. It also means that you want to learn something, and hopefully that you are able to eat, however badly. If, on top of all this, you have the determination to make something of your life, then you must give it a go. If you are a professional person, or trained in the creative sense, then this section probably does not apply to you, unless you are so bad at it that you cannot get work. In any case, you must start, and start now. The clock is running even for you. The only way you are going to put your foot on the ladder is by finding something that people want to buy, if possible something that you can make with your own hands, or if not you then your girl or boy-friend, your mother or the man in the pub.

The place to start is in the markets, Portobello Road or Petticoat Lane for Londoners or your local equivalents. You probably cannot afford the cost of a proper stall. No matter. Just put your product over your arm or in a wheelchair or whatever suits, and walk about and try and sell it. If you sell nothing, then listen to your customers, and come back next week with something else. If you do not fancy the markets, or your product is not right for them, take a tour around the local shops. At this stage, even if you do not make a sale, at least you will learn why not – which, to me, is the most important knowledge you can have. If you are living in a vacuum, you have no chance. Most successful ideas do not happen overnight. The cliché from the more genuine of our super-stars, 'It has taken me 15 years to become an overnight success', is probably an understatement. It disguises all the hard work, the failures, and again the dedication and persistence that they have endured in that very long time.

The difference between success and failure is only a matter of fact. I know two knighted millionaires who nearly went to jail within the last ten years, but they fought it out and made it. So must you.

2

Where did the Money go? – Buying and Controlling

This is a question that will be frequently asked of you by accountants, investors, partners and wives and, if things go really wrong, receivers. What appears to be a very adequate amount of working capital can quickly disappear if you are not completely in control not only of the day-to-day cost of running your business, but also of the future commitments that are being made on your behalf.

We will look at buying first. When you place an order for the product of a person or company, you are in fact making a commitment that you will have to pay for in the future. You must therefore be certain that what you will receive is what you want, both in quality and quantity, and that at the lowest level of anticipated income you will be able to pay for it somewhere around the due date.

It is as essential, therefore, that you control the order book, as much as you do the chequebook, and that each of your employees knows that items arriving, however urgent or necessary, will, unless ordered on your specific instructions, result in their instant dismissal. This may sound tough, but there is no room for compromise. Either you are in control or you are not, and if not you might as well put all your money in a bucket and let them help themselves.

The average trading company spends over 50% of its total income on stock that it has consciously bought in the belief that it is absolutely necessary to its existence. Let us therefore look at some basic rules that you must apply.

Do you really need it, and if so, how much do you need? The first question should be reasonably simple to answer but the reply to the second is not always that easy. The temptation is to buy more than you really need for a particular time-span. Your decision is very often dominated not by what you want but what you can get, when you can get it, and how much it will cost. Most important of these is when can you get it, i.e. what is the lead time, or gap between your order and its arrival at your back door? Clearly, if a supplier takes three months to deliver an item for which you have a current need, then you have to order at least four months estimated requirement to ensure that you do not run out. This means that at the moment of delivery you are going to be in possession of much more of that item than you need for your immediate operations and you are going to have to pay for it long before you sell it. You have therefore created for yourself a stock that, although showing on your books as a net current asset, had taken hard cash out of your business.

In many trades or industries, particularly those involving low-cost items, there is a minimum order below which it is not worth your supplier setting up his machinery to produce. Whatever your needs, you are stuck with this minimum, which can often mean that you are lumbered for the time being with more than you actually need, and again the money goes out, not because you want it to, but because it has to if you are to operate.

The third compelling reason for over-ordering, for that is what you are doing in the financial sense, is the quantity discount. To be competitive in the market you may well have priced your product on the assumption that sales will be much larger than they turn out. There is nothing you can do about it once it has happened, but if the fact that you now need a smaller quantity makes your buying price higher you may often have to finance the difference to preserve your profit margin or else discontinue the line, which can be a very hard decision to make.

Not only does an excessive or uneven stockholding, however unavoidable, mean that you are going to need extra capital in order to pay for it, but it exposes you to two other assessments that only you as the Boss can possibly make. These are:

(a) Are your forecasts of the money coming in to your company so accurate that these extra sums will be there when needed?

(b) Will the excess stock still be as hot in three or four months time as it is when you make your commitment? If not you can find yourself in a very bad situation, when you have a warehouse of yesterday's sellers and no money to buy what you need for today. In order to survive you have to start unloading at any price, and that is usually a fraction of what you paid. I have seen many firms, particularly in the fashion industry, completely stymied in this situation. If they unload they will be legally bankrupt and if not they won't sell anything. They have had it.

This dilemma is most easily encountered when you are dealing with the Far East. In many industries you are forced to buy from the Orient because that is the only place where you can get the value for money that can make you competitive. In order to achieve this value you are entering into the worst of all worlds – long lead times, high minimum quantities, payment usually by Letter of Credit and extended and costly lines of communications and control. Unless you are an extremely wealthy genius with the luck of the devil one day you will come unstuck.

Ideally, all your suppliers should hold stock, and you should be able to send a van down once a day to pick up only what you need for that day. This situation rarely exists, but in principle you are far better off paying a premium to buy what you want when you want it than having too much. Before you decide upon a supplier, process or type of material to be used weigh up these factors of cost, lead time and quantity, and if the equation does not give a commercial answer that you can support, think again. It is easy to change your mind before you start, but once things are rolling practical considerations obscure the true issue and it can be very hard to alter direction.

Suppliers

As important as how you buy is whom you buy from. Here is where the Yellow Pages simply do not work. You need to know much more about a company than the mere fact that it is in the line of business that you need. If you are entering into a commitment to buy a product or service it is because you need it at a given moment, at the quality, price and quantity that you expected, and if you are in a repeat business you need it more than once. What you need is both reliability and flexibility, so that if something changes from the plan – components arrive late or the specification alters for reasons beyond your control – your supplier has both the capacity and willingness to adjust to the new circumstances. The only way you are going to find out the true calibre of your potential resource is to ask around and profit from the experience of others. Few people will give you the name of their best contact. Why should they? They could easily have taken years to discover, through very expensive trial and error and can reasonably be classed as a Trade Secret. Conversely though, all but your closest competitors will be only too pleased to tell you who not to use, even if only to get their own back for past unpleasantness. With any luck, you will end up with a list of names, possibly very short, of firms that check out reasonably cleanly.

Do not then start to write long letters explaining what you want. Ring them up and go and see them, and make sure that you are seeing the person who will be in direct control of your order. It is pointless talking to the Sales Director if the key person for you is in charge of production. Except in really large or monolithic organizations you should be speaking to the Boss. If he is too busy or cannot be bothered to see you, he is giving you a bad impression, which you should heed. At this stage you have lost nothing by parting company, except your time, so if you do not get the right feeling from your visit, go somewhere else. Do not, however burn your boats – you may need them a year from now, or the others on your list may be even worse.

What are you looking for in a supplier? On the assumption that the company has the technical ability and staff to do the work you need, the key factor is attitude. Do they really want your business? They for their part are probably going to be involved in spending time and money in readying your sample or specification for production, and, if you are prudent, your first order will be the minimum possible so that you can test their abilities without incurring too much risk. So your interest in them can be a mixed benefit, and it is as important for you to endear your company to them as vice versa. Don't forget that they are seeing people like you all day long and have suffered their fair share of over-optimistic idiots.

Areas for you to avoid are:

(a) Technical knowledge that you do not possess. There is no reason at all why you the buyer should have any more than the sketchiest idea of the processes involved in the manufacture of your product. Their expertise is part of what you are buying, and nothing annoys technicians more than having some ignoramus telling them what to do. What they usually like is to show off their knowledge, so here you can both please them and learn a bit yourself at the same time.

(b) Giving the impression of wealth or credit rating that is wildly over the top. They can and will check you out, if they have not already done so. It will also encourage them to do a harder deal in terms of price and quantity than otherwise might be the case. There is nothing wrong in being small, or new, or both, if you can demonstrate that you know what you are doing, and that you have a fair chance of success.

(c) Bosses who are so preoccupied with the day-to-day running of their own business that they are not business-men at all, just Production Managers who happen to own the place. If things go wrong from your end they will tend to adopt a peevish 'you let me down' stance that will get in the way of a solution. If they drop you in it, they can become so insulted at your lack of understanding of their problems that diplomatic relations break down at an early stage, leaving you wondering what to do next.

(d) Bosses or companies that are too busy. You neither know nor care how well the other man is doing, or the problems caused by his success or expansion, or the fact that he went public yesterday and is now a millionaire. Good luck to him, but all you are interested in is what he is able to do for you. By the same token a company that is obviously very quiet indeed should attract equal suspicion, for the opposite reasons.

(e) Bosses who talk too much. I do not mean those who ring you up every couple of months for a chat and to see how things are going, but the inveterate rabbiter. You never know if their call is serious or just a waste of half an hour. In the end, you will start avoiding them, and when catastrophe strikes you will not bother to ring back.

(f) Above all Bosses who try to snow you with science, or use the excuse of vast orders from others for the lateness of your own delivery. What happens inside other people's businesses is of no interest to you. You have your own problems, and that should be enough.

25

Running Costs

The average business will spend another 30 to 40% of its income on its running costs, its 'fixed overhead' as it is known. Do not allow the word 'fixed' to fool you – there is little static about it and the one thing that you can rely upon is that it will increase unless you control it yourself, with a fist of steel.

If you make a bad decision and lose money as a result, then it is your fault, but at least you have lost your own cash, and have not allowed someone else to do it for you. Usually the cause and effect is plain for you to see and you can live to fight another day, but your running costs are the enemy from within and are much more insidious and much harder to pinpoint. You must control not only yourself and your own spendthrift ways, but also those of your employees and quite possibly of your own family. Otherwise you will meet death by a thousand petty cash slips, of receipts that have gone missing, expenditures that are unnecessary or excessive, the 'don't spare the ship for a ha'p'orth of tar' syndrome. These halfpennies add up, and as they belong to you, you must make yourself aware of their overall effect.

Your staff live to spend your money – not steal it, just use it. Your paper-workers will surround themselves with a year's supply of everything they can possibly use up, and if you count the soap you'll find that someone has done you a favour and bought you £80's worth at half price. That, depending on your size, can be a lot of soap, and so it goes on.

So what do you do? First make sure that if anybody is going to be wasting money it is you. Second make a realistic budget with separate headings for everything that you think you might have to spend, from the largest to the smallest, rent and rates to milk and coffee, and every time a cost occurs, allocate it to its correct heading. If that starts to go over budget find out why, and either increase your budget, if it is incorrect, or cut back, but do not let the situation continue and do nothing.

In the same way that you must personally sign all orders to your suppliers, you must also be the one who authorizes even the lowliest of expenditures. Some people, who would have you committed if you asked them if they would give you £50 per week to spend on their behalf, will happily OK many times that amount in a week simply because the account balances and all the vouchers are correctly signed. By that time it is too late. You must authorize *all* outgoings before they occur. However petty or boring it may seem, at the end of the year you can be looking at very large amounts of cash represented by filing cabinets (half empty), unused typewriter ribbons and other useless items. Not only have you paid for them, but, if you are in profit, you will have to pay Corporation Tax on them as if they were cash in the bank.

When you are running a smallish business, do not even have a petty cash box. Make people ask you for it, and if you cannot spare it at the moment, too bad. It is amazing what people do not need if they have to ask you personally for the money. This no doubt sounds petty and nit-picking to you if you are a newcomer to proprietorship, but if you have been around a while you will know the truth, particularly if you are running a shop or restaurant, where half your day is spent in the preservation of your property from staff and public alike.

Let us talk about theft for a moment. This is one of the most depressing aspects of owning a company. People steal from you. Respectable, ordinary people who would not dream of stealing from your house or car or the blind man on the corner, will think nothing of shifting a load of your merchandise, food or products into their pockets, even when it has little value to anyone but yourself.

As an ex-shopkeeper and restaurant owner I can speak with great and heart-felt authority on this subject. In Biba, which had the image of a thieves paradise, we managed to keep the direct theft to around 2% of turnover, as opposed to a multiple store's target of 1%, and this was not bad going at the time, as we were averaging the biggest sales per square foot in the world. One of our would-be competitors, a boutique section of a department store, was actually running at over 18%. However, that 2% was an actual £100,000 a year, which is a large amount even today, and was worth much more in the early 1970s. On top of that was the cost to us of keeping it at that level. Security guards, plain clothes store detectives and a percentage of the staff whose job was basically one of surveillance. I am sure that the electronic tags and closed circuit TV of today have done little to solve the problem. If anything staff have become too reliant upon them,

27

and their own vigilance and awareness of what is going on have lost their edge.

There are three basic types of shoplifter. The first is the professional gangs, who may or may not steal to order. These are mostly efficient teams, who concentrate their efforts in the larger, more crowded stores. They are extremely hard to spot and even harder to convict. It is pointless becoming paranoid about them because they are a fact of life, and if yours is a smallish shop they probably will not bother you.

The professional pickpocket, 'steal anything that can't be traced' gangs, cause a different type of problem for the shopkeeper. They arrive mob-handed, steal every purse in sight and disappear before the hue and cry. We had two such groups who used to visit Biba regularly. A shop girl would arrive at the control point with a furious customer who had just lost her bag, or probably just her purse. This was bad news for us, because we knew that we could easily have fifty plus complaints like this in the next five minutes, and that the gang was already far away and impossible to trace. We then would have to go through the whole rigmarole of police and statements and hysteria, all to no point at all.

The folk story was that these gangs were basically Brazilian. They started their annual migration by picking pockets in Sao Paulo railway station to get the fare to Rio, and thence pick their way around Europe, in the tourist season, returning home after three or four months as rich men. Believe it or not, I was once sitting in a bar in Sao Paulo, and fell into conversation with a nice man who knew the European store scene much better than I. 'Have you ever heard of Biba', I asked.

'My God,' he said in the vernacular, 'what a store, what fortunes were lost when it closed.' He peered at me, and slapped me on the shoulder, 'Have I not seen you before Sir?' I admitted it was possible. 'Sir, then you will know, the workers there were hard, but the customers easy.' He put his arm round my shoulder, and laughed at the memory.

If you own a shop, do not worry too much about the so-called professionals. Whatever they take will be a small percentage of the whole. Far more costly is the enthusiastic amateur. They are there each and every day of your life. Some of them may be

28

mentally sick – the apologists call them that, or blame the store for making theft too easy. (I never heard a bank robber using that excuse. 'I am sorry my Lord, but that Natwest was just too easy, so I fell into bad ways.' Try that one and they will give you another five years for insulting their intelligence.) Shoplifters, en masse, are responsible for a huge percentage of total robberies, not only in the UK but world wide, and the poor old shopkeeper is fighting with his hands tied behind his back, as the average magistrate simply does not treat shoplifting as a serious offence and the penalties are frequently laughable.

It is a constant and recognized statistic that in retail establishments *two thirds* of the total pilferage comes from your own staff – the people you pay and look after more or less, and who are there smiling and cheerful every morning. If you don't believe me, ask a shopkeeper. Your problem is that you have to trust someone, somewhere, but whom and where? If you own a restaurant the staff problem is multiplied enormously. 'Perks' are built into that business, but where the bunce stops and theft begins is an area without boundary, and a large part of your time is spent trying to keep your losses within reasonable limits.

Here is a small tale to summarize what for me is the general attitude to the theft of merchandise as against money. I have always thought that, as a retailer, you are in fact hanging £50 notes on your rails, not goods for sale, and this incident confirmed that belief.

When Biba closed we lived in Brazil for about five years, and soon after we came back we were entertained by a very grand lady who had been a friend and customer for many years. The conversation turned, as it sometimes does, to the past. 'Of course,' said the lady, 'you were robbed of so much in that store, all my friends used to take things, even my children did it. You still have some of those things, don't you darlings?' Her children, now over twenty, simpered and nodded.

Barbara and I were both starting to feel well pleased by this revelation. I said, 'You know, it's really funny you should say that. I was in your house at one of your parties just before we left and I found a diamond bracelet on the floor where the coats were. It fetched nearly £2,000 in Brazil.'

They stared at me, mouths open, cheeks flushing.

29

'What,' they roared. 'You stole something from this house? How dare you!' The son said he would call the police. They were stunned by my admission.

'Don't you see', I said, 'that is just what you have told me. Your kids and your friends stole from Barbara and me, and you thought that very amusing.' They could not see it though, it could never cross their minds that theft is theft. We were leaving anyway and never saw them again. In a way, I wish I had found a bracelet. It would have served them right.

3

Cash Flow and Credits

A cash flow is a way of demonstrating on paper the anticipated movement of money in and out of your business, usually week by week or month by month, thus demonstrating exactly how much money you will have, or not have, at any given moment. It is of great importance not only to you but also to any potential lender and is absolutely crucial if you are trying to persuade your bank to give you an overdraft.

The idea is simple enough. You write down your anticipated income, making allowances for late payments, and deduct your outgoings – fixed overheads, payments to suppliers, sales commissions etc. – and there, before your eyes, you have a projection of your cash situation, monthly, weekly, or even daily if you want to make a meal of it, for the period that you are covering.

Banks, in particular, tend to view these things with great scepticism. They are well aware that they are being shown figures designed to encourage them to lend you money and clearly you are not going to present a situation showing your cause to be hopeless. If your accountant is of the 'creative' variety he can show you how to make the same set of numbers demonstrate almost anything you like, but be sure that somewhere in your drawer you have your own personal calculations, and that these are as pessimistic or realistic, whichever shows the worst picture, as you can make them. For heaven's sake, do not try to fool yourself.

If you have an overdraft, your bank will want to see the accounts every six months, together with a cash flow for the same period ahead. Your accountant, if you have paid him, will help you do the figures and will be able to demonstrate, depending on the pressures of the monent, either a) that everything is fine, so that the bank does not start to smell a rat and ask for a reduction of the current borrowing, or b) that the business is expanding, diversifying or coming into a seasonal flat patch (you haven't had an order for 6 weeks, something went wrong with the last deliveries, and no one will pay up, or maybe your biggest customer just went bust) and that it would be prudent for the overdraft to be increased by £5,000, £10,000, or £100,000 depending on your altitude. The bank rarely falls for option b) but at least it stops them taking the unthinkable step of actually reducing your overdraft. If this should happen, get your figures typed out nicely, and on your bike to any banks with whom you have not already fallen out, full of plausible reasons for needing a change.

The fact is that this 'official' cash flow, probably propping up a cheerful looking profit and loss projection, is inevitably absolute rubbish. It presupposes that you can correctly forcast your sales by product, colour, or whatever you are dealing in, that your suppliers will deliver on time and most important of all, when your customers will pay you. If you as a newish or smallish business can be 70% right on your forecasts, you are doing very well indeed, which gives you the other 30% of grey area to be overcome.

Unless you have access to a massive amount of cash/capital in relation to your size of operations this grey area is going to occupy the best part of your time and energies. You are lucky if you're only worrying about what is going to happen four weeks ahead. Normally your problems are right on your shoulder, frequently only a few days away, and this is when you personally really start to earn your money. What you do *now* is what is going to determine the course of your life, and only you can do it. What triumphs you had yesterday are out of the window and tomorrow will not come if you do not do something today. Your problem is that you do not have readies. You have stock, you have orders, and maybe even profits, but the barter system went out with the Romans. You cannot pay the staff in lipstick or dresses or fluffy toys. They want actual money and they want it the day it is due. So do your landlord, your wife, and probably the man at the garage. With the rest you have some latitude, and this is the game you have to play.

Basically you have two types of supplier – the irreplaceable and the expendable. It is critical that you are on good, first-name terms with the owners, Chief Accountant or whoever of the former. If you have been wise you will have built up a spasmodic payment pattern, a bit here a bit there and a sudden out-of-the-blue payment if you think you are flush that week, so that they are never expecting to receive a set amount on a set day. Even if you have the money never pay the full amount on the due date. It sets a precedent that they will seize upon for ever after. Do not get the reputation of being a good payer. Of course you can't be too bad or they won't deliver, and then you are in real trouble. You will notice that the pressure for payment increases as their delivery dates to you draw closer, as the leverage is on their side and things can get very sticky. This situation must be avoided. Above all you must either talk to them or find a remarkably good reason not to. Remember that you can only make a miraculous recovery from a terminal illness every so often before it starts to look a bit thin.

Here is where your entrepreneurial skills really count. It is not only what you say, but when you say it that scores. It is no good telling a man who is expecting a cheque for £10,000 tomorrow that due to an oversight in your Accounts Department you have paid someone else instead of him and he will have to wait until a cheque from Singapore which was sent yesterday gets cleared through your bank. He will go mad, particularly if he knows that you *are* the Accounts Department. No, you have to soften him up. Tell him ten days in advance that you will pay him without fail on such and such a day. Drop the Singapore cheque into the conversation, tell him it is on its way, imply the 10 days will give ample time for the clearance and so on. If he is half bright he will already start to get that sinking feeling, but you have got him on the hook he, willy nilly, has become involved in your problems, whether he likes it or not, and you can play him along happily for another two or three weeks before it's hand in pocket time. There are endless variants on this theme, and you probably know more than I do, but it is very wearing both for you and for your staff, and the assistance of a moderately able person is essential if the full gambit of ploys and manoeuvres is to be worked properly.

Larger companies are able to employ a far more subtle and elaborate pattern of evasion, and it can be very hard to beat. I was once trying to collect a cheque from a television company. It was not for much, but the shifts and turns that impeded the payment were a lesson to us all. First there was a half-hour wait to be connected to Accounts. My first call found a very nice girl who went away to look for the invoice. I could hear background laughter and teacups, and finally she came back to say that everything was all right. She had found the invoice and would pass it for payment. I explained that it was already four weeks late. She repeated that everything was all right now. Two weeks later I rang again. Same performance, different girl, only this time no invoice. Sent copy, rang a week later, invoice received and sent 'upstairs' for approval. Beautiful, the invoice was now in a hallowed and impenetrable place and its future had nothing to do with the people I had been speaking to. We were paid finally three months late. The lesson is that larger companies will pay you when it damn well pleases them and if you don't like it you know what to do. Compared to Europe the English are bad payers, but against the USA and other third world countries they are marvellous. I will come back to that later, but all in all things could be worse.

Back to the small company without these massive resources for prevarication. The person who answers the telephone is critical to your financial image. This does not mean that they have to be of the Sloane persuasion, probably the reverse, although a bright, properly motivated gel, of whom there are a few, can be a major asset. The important thing is that they are either smart enough to say exactly what you tell them to or so stupid or incoherent or both that whatever they say will cause the maximum confusion at the other end. I have a tremendously good combination at the moment. One is a nice lad who is more or less catatonic. It takes him over a minute to get a word out, so he is always answering the wrong question. He is the B team, the back up. The A team is a lovely girl who is Finnish. Her understanding of English is extremely good but she can if she likes become dyslexic and discordant, particularly if she gets excited or nervous. Business-owning friends of mine are deeply impressed. Answering machines are also a major weapon and have been known to reduce strong men to tears.

The point is that although your main line of defence is in talking to people, there are times when there is absolutely nothing that you can say to them that will do any good at all. They want an answer. When will they get paid? The 'What can I say to you?' approach can be on occasions very effective, but not in the context of a continuing relationship.

What you must never do is tell direct lies – never, never, never. Do not say the cheque is in the post, do not say you *will* be paid next week unless you are absolutely certain that it is going to happen. You are much better off saying 'I cannot pay you this week', or even 'this month' than getting them all excited and committed to payments of their own on the back of your imaginary cheque.

Time

There are various soporifics that you can give to avert what at this stage is the ultimate breakdown of relationships, the writ. As I will explain in another section, what you are looking for is time. Most writs, although not the end of the world, start to give a predictable scale to a forced moment of payment. There are ways around this too, but they are very worrying and worry is what you must seek to avoid, as it will eat up your energy, imagination and will to survive.

Most companies who are knocking on the door are in the same state as you are. They can't pay the wages/the rent/the wife has been unable to cash her housekeeping cheque. They are up to their necks in it. What do they need? Anything they can get their hands on. They are starving. You will find that at weekends, when the wages are due and the Boss and wife are going to the golf club, drag-hunt or the Hackney dogs, the need for cash in hand becomes critical. You have the same pressures of course, but the wise punter will have kept something back for this purpose. If you owe the man £2,000 and can give him £300 cash and a few post-dated cheques for the rest, he will be your friend for life. You can spin him out for a long long time, but *be careful* – these things come home to roost.

Documentary Credits

As your business expands, particularly if you are involved in buying or selling overseas, you will come across another form of credit which, unless you know what you are doing, can be

35

extremely dangerous. These are known as Documentary Credits, the most common of which are Bills of Exchange and Letters of Credit. This is what they are and what you should be watching for.

Bills of Exchange

These are simple little things which look just like oversized cheques, but they are dynamite, particularly if you are an importer. Somehow the Europeans take them to be like cash in the bank. They can discount them, get credit from them and generally think that they have you well stitched up. Frequently the B of X, as we nervously call it, will get you about ten times the credit that you would normally expect without it. The snag is that, unlike sending a post-dated cheque around the houses, your bank takes a similar view. You can always stop a cheque if you cannot pay it and the bank will think no less of you, but a B of X is different. Your whole creditibility goes down the drain. In England it is known as an absolute document – there is no argument against it. You cannot say that you never had the goods, that they are defective, late or unordered – all the old excuses are swept away and you can go to the cleaners remarkably quickly if you do not cough up on the due date, and your bank will pay them ahead of any cheques due that day. On the other hand, they are legal documents and you can always use this to your advantage. I have paid out about £250,000 over the last two years to a component supplier in Germany by this method. Thank heavens I have the money to pay them, but I have signed each one in a way that makes them illegal. Every time they are presented the bank rings up and asks, 'Do you really want to pay this?' So far my answer is yes, but maybe one day the 'grey area' will be upon me, and I will say no. Life is full of sudden death situations and you need a little insurance.

Letter of Credit

If I can give you one piece of advice it would be *never* get involved in a Letter of Credit. It can happen to you even without your knowledge or consent and you will always regret it. It is the most exacting financial document that you will ever come across and is interpreted differently both from country to country and between banks within countries.

If you are an exporter or importer or both, you will inevitably be trading with overseas commpanies whose only method of dealing is through this docummency. So, if you really have to do it let me give you a simplified set of rules plus some of my own experience in this area.

The rules first – the L/C you accept as a seller must be:

(a) Irrevocable
(b) Transferable
(c) Part deliveries must be accepted
(d) There must be no pre-shipment inspection clause
(e) It must be F.O.B., i.e. delivered to a shipping agent at your local airport on or before the due date. It means Free on Board, and the ins and outs of it are explained later.

It may well seem here that I am talking down to you, but I have seen so much money lost through this route, and having myself shipped several millions of dollars over five years from Brazil to the western world I ought to know.

Letters of Credit are based on documents, not facts and not merchandise. They normally are paid automatically from the bank of the sender on presentation of the correct paperwork. Now consider what that means. The bother of opening an L/C is only justified if we are talking about big amounts. If you are in a small way of business this could well be your biggest ever order. The one that will change the world. The documents required are normally the invoice, airway bill or bill of lading, packing list and sometimes certificate of origin, and the whole thing is based on the delivery date. This means that if you arrive with £100,000 of merchandise at 0.01 of the day after, the whole L/C is invalid. Something to think about.

Let us now go back to the basic rules,

(a) If it is not irrevocable it is worthless.

(b) If it is not transferrable you cannot pass a part of it onto someone else, probably a supplier, and then you are locked into the terms of the L/C and the supplier is not – they can deliver a load of rubbish, or deliver late or both and the local law will apply, not the exacting demands of the L/C.

(c) If you are not allowed part deliveries you may have 80% of the order ready on the due date, but no part deliveries means no payment and you will be stuck with the lot. When we were trying to buy back the Biba name and cosmetic company one of the sticking points that I could not wear was an order backed by an L/C from Iran, at the time of the Shah, for £150,000, which everybody on the British side insisted on treating as if it had been paid for in cash, and they wanted me to pay face value for the order. I could not accept that, and I was right. They had no part delivery clause in the L/C, they shipped about £110,000, the L/C went down and the man didn't pay. QED.

(d) You, the seller, cannot under any circumstances agree to a pre-shipment inspection clause. It effectively invalidates the L/C, and can be used by the unscrupulous either to cancel orders they no longer want or to put you in a position where you have to take almost any price for the goods you are stuck with.

By the same token you must never buy with a Letter of Credit. Firstly, unless you are biggish and popular with your bank the money will be debited to your account the moment that the L/C is issued. As far as you are concerned you are giving cash with order, and if you are using your resources correctly the cash will not be there anyway. It is a non starter. However, if there is no way out, and you have to issue an L/C you *must* insert a preshipment inspection clause. This, as the buyer is your big let out – a certificate of quality as part of the payment document, but the inspection must be carried out by you or your most trusted person. There are world wide networks who will do it for you, and who normally take a percentage of the value involved, but avoid them at all costs unless you are sure that their man on the spot knows what he's doing. Don't forget, they are inspecting on your behalf merchandise that you have ordered, to your specification. The people doing the checks have never seen you, or your business, and have quite likely never been involved in your area of activity.

We were shipping around $500,000 worth of T-shirts from Brazil to Italy in 1976. We were new to the third world but we were not stupid, nor was the owner of the factory that was producing the goods. Everything was set. Merchandise sold, sealed samples OK'd and at $1.50 a shot, it was plenty of T-shirts. Suddenly the L/C arrives and in comes the man from the inspection agency. He was probably typical of the kind of person that will be working for you if you are silly enough to use one. He was a bureaucrat, and had spent his whole life checking crates of coffee for lumps of rock – coffee being sold by weight, you tend to get a large rock content. He had a thick wad of regulations, and he took a fabric sample away to the laboratory for testing. He came back three days later, to say that on a one to 10 count we scored 9. So our fabric had failed. There was a panic meeting with the factory, and with the inspection agency. What he did not know was that in Brazil 10 is the best possible rating. This was a bad start, but things quickly became worse. The man had a book of garment size measurements that must have been taken from the Amazons and completely distorted the shape of the designs; he had a set of labelling instructions that were pre-EEC and therefore obsolete; he had misread the packing instruction so that we ended up with boxes off assorted styles and colours – impossible to distribute without repacking. We gave him drinks, bribes, free samples for his wife, but he was obdurate. We finally received his certificate, shipped the delivery and we were paid by the bank. Our customer had to repack over 300,000 items that would fit a gorilla all because *his* inspector did not know what he was doing.

4
Selling

Whether you have a product, service or shop, sales are what it is all about, and although what I am going to tell you is best exemplified in terms of a product most parts apply equally well to the other two.

Basic Research

I do mean basic. You have no need or money to spare to employ experts. If you cannot do it for yourself, then you are not cut out for this business or probably any other. Fundamentally you must believe that there is a reason why your potential customers will wish to buy your product and not those of others in the field.

These reasons have to be all or some of the following:

You are (a) Unique
         (b) Better
         (c) Cheaper
         (d) Faster
         (e) More efficient

If you are unique, it depends how unique and for how long. However well protected by patents you may think you are, if you really have discovered something that is the first of its kind and there is a demand for it, the big boys will be on your tail at once, and unless you are able to compete on one or more of the other areas I have mentioned, you will be out of the business. Being first is a mixed advantage and very often people find themselves breaking ground and doing market research for others, who learn from the mistakes they make and come in and mop up afterwards.

The way things are, although you are small as you start up, you will be competing with the giants from day one. You will be after the same counter-space, distributors or consumer pound that many firms are spending millions of pounds to secure. All you have against their vast array of cash and expertise is yourself and

40

your ideas, and you should have no illusions that because you are just starting up anyone is going to do you a favour. You must be absolutely certain that you are offering something that is wanted, that you are going to be able to produce it at a profit while remaining competitive in price, and that your first orders are going to be properly produced and on time.

The best research is to study the competition. You may well think that their product is second rate, their price excessive and their design content zero, but they are in business and have been for some time, maybe in a very large way. Think hard about why this is. It is highly unlikely that you are going to make them obsolete overnight, so you are going to have to find your niche alongside them and offer very good reasons to the store buyer or whoever will be giving you your first orders, why you should be there at all.

The best way is to go and ask, rather than sell. If you are lucky this might happen, but simply go and ask a cross section of your potential customers what they think of your product. The average buyer of anything is only too delighted to tell you why they will *not* place an order, and at an early stage of your product development and business stratagem this can be more useful than an order for half a dozen or ten gross or whatever denominations you deal in. At least if you know what is not wanted you know what to avoid.

Do not trust the opinion of any one person. You must see several, in the various avenues of distribution that you think you may cover. Even then, do not take what they say as gospel, but store it and use it later, if needs be as a weapon against them. Few buyers really know the broader aspects of the trade that they are in. Their vision is usually limited to what happened last week. Even journalists, who are meant to have a wider view of the world, rarely leave their offices, and go out to see what is going on. We showed my wife's first small collection to a journalist who was a big power in her day. She gave us the horse laugh and six months later we were the hottest thing in fashion and she was out of a job. Unfortunately, if you are going through the normal distribution channels, you have to deal with these people. Quite often the decision is not theirs anyway, but they are the filter to the powers above and if you cannot get past them, you will not get anywhere. You must know what they are looking for and tailor your product, price and service accordingly.

Beware the advice you are getting however, particularly if it is positive. People who are not being asked to commit money at the moment may genuinely think they are doing you a favour if they enthuse about your product or plans, which can be much more damaging than the wet blanket. This happened to me almost three years ago. We were starting a new product with a new company. I saw one of the biggest buyers in that field, and she went over the top about the samples.

'When will you be able to deliver?' I told her. 'Come back in six weeks and we'll do the order.' She was really excited and, so was I. Five weeks later I rang for an appointment. After 15 years with that company she had just left to start a business selling bath taps. The new buyer would not even talk to me. 'Serves you right,' you say. So it did, but it was a big blow at the time. As the Boss, that was when I earned my money, and we got over it, but I should never have put myself in that position of relying heavily on one customer in the first place – nor must you.

It all comes down in the end to commonsense and an understanding of the real world that you will be up against once you start to go for the money. I can assure you that, having subjugated your drive and enthusiasm to these degrading discussions, you will start to have the most severe doubts as to why you ever had the idea in the first place. It is better for you to go through this trauma before you are fully committed than at a later stage when your boats are charred and useless.

Selling

Many people who know no better regard the art of selling as being both demeaning and unnecessary, and look upon the salesperson as a drone on society and generally not nice to know. How often have you heard the dismissive 'Oh, he (or she) is just a salesman'? As you should know, or will quickly learn, a good salesperson is worth their weight in gold and should be treated accordingly. Your problem in starting up with an unknown and untried product is to find such a person. Early on this is often not possible, and you will find yourself with your bag of samples sitting for hours in waiting-rooms, surrounded by hordes of others all bearing bags and suitcases, and you will be wondering what on earth you are doing there. Probably quite rightly – the odds are that you are waiting to see the wrong person anyway, or at least someone who has no intention at all of placing an order at what to them is at best a sounding out, but to you may be a matter of survival.

A good salesman has been through all this years ago. He will have established a relationship with everyone of any importance in his field. He will know the decision makers and how to reach them, know when they are open to buy and when just passing the time of day. He should know all the trade gossip, who likes and who loathes whom, who is on the move and what jobs are on offer. He is not only the buyers' contact with your company, he is also a window to the outside world. Both are equally necessary to each other. Without one, the other would not exist.

By representing your company the salesman has implicitly guaranteed your quality and reliability. He cannot afford to be associated with an inferior product or it will reflect upon him and his reputation, which is his stock in trade. So, conversely, you should be very careful of representatives who seek to work for you at an early stage unless you know them, either personally or by reputation, very well indeed.

There are four main types of representation that you should consider before deciding how best to operate. They all have a part to play in the scheme of things. They all have advantages and disadvantages and much depends on the general practice of the trade that you are in. Normally you can only select one route or another. If you try to get the best of too many worlds you are likely to upset everybody – you have two salesmen calling on the same buyers, exclusive arrangements with two stores in the same street and arguments about who gets what commission until everyone is sick of the sound of your name and you are in danger of losing the lot.

The basic categories are:
(a) *Full or part time salespeople, employed directly and only by yourself*
At first glance this may seem the most logical way to go. You are in control of your people and you think you know what they are

doing all day long. Their loyalty is only to you, and your company is a self contained entity, totally self reliant.

However, salespeople are expensive. If they work only for you there is the cost of their transport, their telephone bills, expenses for entertaining customers and other bits and pieces of legitimate expenditure. Their remuneration will have to be a mixture of fixed salary plus commission, which is fine as long as things are going well, but your sales people have to eat every day, and if you have a seasonal bias to your business that means that half the time you are giving hand-outs, because through no fault of anyone's the business is simply not there. Then when the season does come they are working to pay you back, which is bad motivation.

From the salesperson's angle, the disadvantage of representing you alone is that he has only one thing to talk about, unless you are in the type of business, say the fashion trade, that depends upon a whole string of new items three or four times a year. Also, unless you have hundreds and hundreds of small accounts to be visited, there is simply not enough ammunition available to give good reason for close and frequent contact with buyers. So the connection can wither for lack of things to talk about.

Take another case, where your company has, as they say, let the buyer down, perhaps delivered late or part only, or a load of rubbish. Your poor salesperson has no choice but to take the abuse for something that was absolutely not his fault, with no other material to divert the wrath or change the subject. So what do they do? Being human, they probably hide, which means that the entire connection between you and your life's blood is in the lap of the gods and you are in big trouble.

(b) Self-Employed Agents
Here the pros and cons are the exact opposite as for the wholly-employed. Although their commission will be higher you do not have any additional expenses and you only pay them on results. They are carrying other people's, hopefully non-competitive, products, and are spreading their own expenses across them all. They have the entrée to virtually all the accounts in their area. They have built up their own connection, and in your early stages are certainly making much more money than you are, but they are completely outside your personal control.

What happens is the following. As long as they are reasonably successful with their initial selling to the trade, and you on your part have made satisfactory deliveries, they will be on your side. The 5 or 10% that you have added to their earnings will be appreciated, and if the product is moving all will be well. You will have been properly introduced to far more doors than you or your own sales force could possibly manage in a given time and everything should be looking good. Except that, at the first sign of trouble, their natural reaction will be to bail out immediately. At least with your own sales force, however deeply they might bury themselves under the same circumstances, at the end of the month they have to surface, at least to get their wages, and you can lead them back into the fray. As you can see though, it is absolutely not in the best interest of the independent agent to die in a ditch on your behalf – quite the opposite. So if you use them you must be very sure that you are going to be able to perform your part of the action without presenting them with any problems of your making. If you do, or if your product is not quite as easy to sell as everyone imagined, they will disappear into the mist, having taken care not to have dirtied their own nests with their customers by dropping you in it up to your neck. You can lose your business overnight.

(c) The Distributor
Normally speaking you are dealing with a fairly substantial business which will actually buy your product from you and sell it via its own sales force. They will expect a far higher margin than the agent's commission, but you will make savings because you have only one delivery point and receive one large order rather than many lesser ones, and your product will have the backing of a well-organized and probably national sales force.

The disadvantages, however, are enormous. First you are completely in the hands of one company, both for sales and payments. If they have a cash-flow problem so do you, and if they go bust you probably go with them. Furthermore you have absolutely no contact with the outlets to whom they are selling – you do not even know who they are.

Obviously, a distributor is even more cautious than an agent as to whom he will take on, as his commitment is correspondingly greater. If you get in with the right person, and have the wind behind you, all will be well. If things go wrong, though, they really come unstuck, and you can find yourself sitting alone in a warehouse full of your merchandise, with no cash coming in because the distributor won't pay you, no sales force, no knowledge of where your product has been sold and barrow-loads of it on offer at half price in every market in the country, because they have cut their losses and unloaded their stock – and there is nothing that you or your lawyer can do about it.

(d) The Wholesale Warehouse

This can be very important, depending on your line of business. They act to some extent like a distributor, in so far as they buy direct from you, but as their reason for existence is in the supply to the retail trade of a very wide range of normally low cost items, at high frequency – often twice a day in big cities – they tend to concentrate on a fairly limited geographical area. To many types of smaller retailer – chemists, newsagents/tobacconists, hardware and electrical stores are prime examples – they supply a high percentage of their total volume. In essence, where small shops need a very wide selection of merchandise to make a living, the wholesaler carries the stock for them, as this is the only way that they can operate. They have neither the space nor cash to have any depth of stock in any one item, and if you are producing low-cost items aimed at this type of outlet the wholesaler is absolutely essential to your plans.

There are two other ways that you can go, which are more of a marketing decision than a straightforward evaluation of known types of sales structure. They both bypass the old established methods of bringing yourself to the attention of your customers, and both offer an alternative that, if you get it right, is a short cut to success. In my experience they are both of the kamikaze variety, but you should be aware of them.

One is *concessions* or, as it is now being pedalled, the 'Galleria Concept'. Twenty years ago it was called 'Shop within Shop' and I do not remember too much money being made even in those days, when the going was much easier than now. The idea is that you take a small section within a relatively large store and operate it as your own shop. You supply the merchandise and sales staff, and the store will pay you slightly more than the amount you usually charge for your goods, and give you use of space, light, heat, security etc. You will normally only be offered this opportunity if your merchandise is a bit off the beaten track, i.e. the sort of stuff that does not have the broad, mass market appeal and price points that has to be the staple diet of any large department or multiple store. You are selling the jam, they have the bread and butter.

A good deal, you may say to yourself, so why is the store offering it? They will reply that your merchandise is very special, that you know your own market better than they do and that your sales staff have the expertise on your product that theirs lack, and so on and so on until you start to believe in your own unique genius and say yes.

For a start, look very carefully at the type of customers who are coming through the doors, and specifically at those who are passing by the area in which you will be. This is usually catch number 1. Stores are designed and laid out by very clever people to give a certain logical flow to the movement of customers, within which the various key categories of merchandise are placed to maximize the sales of items that are actually owned by the proprietors.

The larger the store, the less controllable the multitude, so you find certain 'dead' areas that the owners find it hard to make profitable. These areas may be dead because no one goes there or because as they are passing through their minds are not actually on buying at that moment. For an extreme example a site in a lift, however many people a day enter and however captive they are as an audience, is useless, because mentally they are in transit, whereas a pitch at the head of the up escalator is excellent, because at that stage they have 'arrived' and their minds are open to suggestion.

That's the first problem. Secondly, your salesgirl, who you are paying, is patrolling an area that in size and therefore merchandise selection is normally much less than that which the store itself would think reasonable. Thirdly, your girl is not one girl, because you have to supply cover for your area at all times. You will certainly need two people, probably two and a half. The store does not have to do this, as they can shuffle their days off etc. so that vast areas are left totally unattended during quiet times.

Fourth, you cannot deliver your vendeuse to the spot and then abandon her. Someone has to go in every day to see what is happening, check the sales, count the stock and supervise. This has to be either you or an extremely able person who must be well paid. Not only do they have to keep up morale and give you an accurate playback of events so that you can adjust your own plans and production etc. but they are going to bear the brunt of all the unpleasantness that this sort of situation engenders. As soon as they arrive, the girl will start moaning about various injustices, the store managers will pounce with suggestions and demands for greater volume of sales and unless very fleet of foot they will be sent upstairs to hang about outside an executive office until someone is free to tell them what you are doing wrong, which normally means putting money into various schemes the store has invented for promoting themselves at your expense.

You multiply this situation a few times, remembering always that the store is only going to pay you your percentage of what you have sold, having deducted everything they can think of, including, if you do not read the small print very carefully, an amount for future markdowns, which comes out of your end and not theirs and which normally mean that you are lucky to retrieve your manufacturing costs, and you are onto a hiding to nothing.

Some people have made it by this route, but only if they are already so big that they can almost dictate their own terms. I know personally one of those and about fifty who lasted for several months before going under. The truth is that the more you make the more the store will demand from you in terms of promotional money and peripheral benefits that will take the fun out of it. They will cane the last 50 pence out of your profit.

I was operating in a department store in New York on a sort of concession basis, and after some months of big sales I could see that I was about to lose money. Barbara and I were lunching with the president of the store, so I asked him, 'How does anyone make money from selling to your store?' He replied, 'You don't, we're X'. He really thought that the promotional value to me of being in his shop was all that I should consider. In his case he had some justification, at the time, but you can ask the same question of Bentalls, Bennetton & Bangers of Berkhampstead, and they will probably all be of the same opinion. Retailers should retail and manufacturers should supply and the transaction should be at arms length – but it never is.

And now for *Mail Order*. Here you have two distinct routes. You sell to another's catalogue, or you do your own. We will take them in order, for reasons that you will see. The mail order industry in the UK is second only to the USA in terms of volume and I would say much more efficient. Britain is a small country, with far too many shops at very high rentals in relation to the available market. Yet mail order continues to hold and even increase its own share of what, door by door, has to be a diminishing volume.

The first route is to sell your product to a catalogue. Contrary to popular belief, the giants do not actually offer any better value than the average multiple shop. What they do offer is selection and credit. This costs them money, so they have to make a mark-up way above that of a typical retailer, whatever their size. To do this and still come in at an acceptable price they screw the supplier in two ways. One, they could not care less what it costs you. They know the selling price and thus work back to what they will pay. Two, they will place an opening order of say 1,000 units, but they have no idea at all what the ultimate sales will be, and I do mean no idea.

I have seen items that I have been involved with, using basically the same photographs, appearing in the same part of the page in two different catalogues and one has sold 30,000 pieces and the other about 500. The buyer will know almost within 5% how much a whole page will take, but has no idea which items the money will come from. Therefore, they pass on the risk to you and so you must pass it on to the suppliers of the components that go into your product.

If Lord Wolfson does not know what is going to sell then you most certainly do not. So you, as he, must lay off the odds, but Lord help you if you cannot support a winner. You will be banned for ever, by everyone in the game. So therefore it's down to your suppliers. If they are not prepared to give you the same commitment that you are giving up front it is hopeless starting and you should forget it.

A good buyer from a major catalogue will know all this, and will buy from a fair spread of merchandise across the section that he deals in, so that your odds of striking lucky are well covered. As soon as you are told that they think it is a winner and here is an order for 500, but you must have 5,000 in stock, either say goodbye or start screaming. They are not trying to bust you, just keep you ticking over, and as long as you realize that you will make some sort of a living, but twice a year you are fighting for survival.

The second option, your own catalogue, is a different matter. I know, because I tried it. The Biba catalogues are in ever-increasing demand from museums, exhibitions and private collectors as one of the greatest examples of commercial photography of the 1960s. Indeed, our catalogues were of great quality. We used the best photographers of the time, and there is seldom a retrospective display from that era that does not include at least one of ours. At the time, every Art Director would have them on the wall above his desk, and in terms of sales they were massive.

As we were producing everything ourselves we had to carry on our backs all the negative elements that the big operators were able to spread around the houses, and very hard to bear they were. We had huge orders, but supplying them in a reasonable time was almost impossible because I, in common with everyone else, could not forecast the sales of any individual item. Every customer would complain on the same day that they had not received their order, so I needed more people on my side to reply to them. In the end I had more people answering queries than I had making dresses. The finale came for me when a blouse that was one of several items on the page, including my Great Danes, and of which only the collar and sleeves showed, sold 14,000 in the first week, which meant not only that we could not supply it quickly, as I had put it down for 1,000 maximum, but that other items that we had in stock did not sell, so we were doubly in the mire.

If it can happen to GUS it will happen to you if you are selling items of the moment, but if you are of the Habitat, non-changing persuasion, where you only have to alter 10% of your product every five years, then consider this route. If you have the cash to stick it out for two or three years you are onto a good thing.

An ultimate thought on your sales policy is that of *bribery*, either in cash or kind. Many, let us even say most of those who really have the power to place large, profitable orders are sitting on goldmines in the Bahamas or Channel Islands and other esoteric places. You may wonder why the old and experienced buyers do not curse the young person who is their boss. The answer is that the last thing the buyers want is promotion, which would take them away from direct contact with their suppliers, the source of all this untaxed and untraceable income. They can be making, in terms of readies, much more than the Chairman, and as long as the company is getting its fair whack, why should anyone care? You will though, and that is why you need your salesperson, as they know how to get the order and jolly things along. It is useless for you, as an outsider, to try and get in on this game. Resist the temptation to run around slipping £50 notes in to the palms of decision makers. You can go to jail for that. This sort of hand-in-pocket relationship takes years to develop and if you really need to sell to these people, find someone who is in the know to act for you or your chances of getting in are NIL.

5

Staff and their Management

Early days

Apart from money, staff are going to be your greatest problem from the moment you hire your first person until you retire to Barbados or Jersey or Carey Street, depending on your aptitude and good fortune. Think extremely carefully before you employ anybody, particularly the first person, and *most* particularly if that first person is going to be of the office administrator/secretary type. This person will be working closely with you, and will reflect the image of the company to the outside world and set the tone of your internal operations and management style for a long time to come. They can quite easily ruin you.

For a start, do you need anyone at all? Unfortunately you probably will in the end – the question is when? There *will* come a moment when there has to be some sort of smokescreen between you and the outside world. You will need someone to answer the telephone in your absence and to deal with all the nitpicking details – the chasing of payments, the queries from other people's accounts departments and hundreds of other minor lunacies that have become necessary in day-to-day business. But do you need them on day one? Hopefully not; all you really need until money starts flowing in is you, a pencil, paper and a telephone. This is particularly hard to grasp, particularly if you already have experience in other people's companies. Your natural instinct is to surround yourself with the trappings that you have been conditioned to associate with power and efficiency.

However, hiring someone costs far more than their basic salary. You have your employer's contribution to the government. They need space in which to sit. Your telephone bill will increase. Suddenly you are constantly running out of petty cash. Even your consumption of basics such as coffee, milk and loo paper goes soaring up and, most dangerous of all, work may be being created more for its own sake than for any good it is doing you, and all of this is costing you *your* money. Resist the moment of hiring your first person for as long as you can – certainly until the business is generating enough gross profit to cover those extra costs.

This is easier said than done, however. Your ego and expectations as 'the Boss' conspire to make you want an instant empire – there isn't much point in being a boss if there is no one to order about. This is absolutely wrong. More mistakes are made in the first few days of euphoric independence than most survivors care to think about. After all, what are you boss of? In reality it is the cheque book. Only you have the power to decide what is going to be paid and when. This is the sole difference between you the employer and you the employee.

The 1987 salary of a Secretary/Administrator has a true cost to you of £15/20,000 p.a., a van and driver £15,000 p.a. and a part time cleaner £2,000 p.a. There you have over £35,000 going out before you get up in the morning. That is nearly £3,000 a month of gross profit down the drain before you have earned a penny, and if you are not making any gross profit on day one of your operation that is £3,000 a month out of your reserves – you can lose money doing that.

Suppose that as a sane and responsible person you have been through all these calculations, and decide that you need and can afford your first employee. Probably you need someone to look after things generally at the base while you are out drumming up business. So who do you hire? For a start I can tell you who not to hire. Go nowhere near friends or their wives/husbands, brothers or sisters, and certainly keep away from your own family. The relationship is just wrong. You need a clean working situation with no other ties so that it can be easily severed if things don't work out.

The problem is that you can go to agencies, have recommendations from business acquaintances and interview until you are black in the face, but you still will not know what you have got until they are sitting looking at you across their desk, and I can only wish you luck. After 20 years of running businesses around the world, I came back to England and found myself in just such a situation. I had hired a woman who was well recommended, experienced in the areas that I needed, reasonably well dressed, married and with a family. Sounds perfect? It was a nightmare – I had put my foot right in it.

For a start, she didn't like the work. Then she *would* keep ringing people up. Reps started arriving to show her things that were of absolutely no relevance to what we were doing. She didn't like selling and she didn't like typing, what she really liked were petty cash and lunch hours. Every time I came back to the office she would say 'You owe me £10' and I would say 'Why?' 'Because a messenger came from X and we ran out of coffee' and so on and so on. The lunch hours rapidly became farcical. She was the life and soul of the local wine bar. Gentlemen started ringing. The lunch hours became longer and longer, the excuses wilder – afternoon telephone calls from the Board of Trade, which had disbanded years before, from the 'BBC TV Studios', where she was apparently fixing us up with a 30 minute documentary, and best of all she once arrived back at 5.30 – she'd forgotten her bag – and announced that the man she had lunched with had suffered a heart attack and she had gone with him to hospital in the ambulance. This one I could well believe. As you can imagine, this arrangement did not last too long, but after she had collected her cards her husband, who was *big*, came round to break my neck, saying that she was 'gutted'. She probably was, but not by me. We can all make these mistakes, and I just hope that you have not or do not. If you have, don't worry about it, get rid of the offending employee quickly and start again.

Let's get onto bigger things. You have survived the first traumas, business is looking up and you are rightly hiring the people that you think you need to go further. You have to think very hard about who you need and why you need them.

The first person to think about is yourself. Apart from owning the company, what are you 'good at'. Maybe nothing at all. Maybe you are a designer, inventor, salesman, production man or administrator – whatever you are you certainly are not all of these put together. By now you have probably become a jack of all trades, which is as it should be as long as you don't get carried away and assume that you know the lot. To have gone as far as you already have you need a fair ration of conceit, but you must have at least an idea of your limitations, and these are the areas into which you must concentrate your future managers. There is a saying that a great salesman makes a lousy Managing Director, and this is probably right, as the necessary optimism of the salesman is exactly what a financial planner does not need, but if you are the salesman *and* the M.D. you had better strengthen your financial controls and forecasting as soon as you can afford to. Never forget, however, that the small business cannot afford to be 100% efficient. In most cases, the cost of the last 10% is out of all proportion to the saving involved.

When you decide that the time has come to take on a financial man, you will find that he wants to put controls on everything, including you. You won't like it, but you must accept it, up to the point when the cost and effort of super-efficiency is getting in the way of your real business – the making of profit. This is why you are the boss and as you introduce more and more specialists into the works you will often have to remind yourself of this. Never forget that they are working to make you money, not you them. Of course you must pay them a decent wage etc., but you must establish from day one who is working for whom. This sounds pretty basic, but they are not thinking that way. They are working for themselves, and if something better comes up they will be off and running. It is a 'you and them' situation and always will be, so don't you forget it.

This brings us up to your management style, which simply means how do you, the boss, get the most out of these people who are eating their heads off at your expense? There are many theories ranging from the 'One Minute Manager' to major works on psychological and industrial motivation. However, it is your life and you must adopt a style that you can live with without strain. It is no good trying to run a company of quiet, industrious, dedicated young people, if you personally are an alcoholic sex maniac with a foul mouth, but on the other hand you do not want any more like you around – you see the problem?

However you decide to pitch it there are a few fundamentals.

(a) Do not be so aloof, or terrifying, or both that your managers cannot stand up to you if they think you are making a mistake. You will make mistakes by the ton, and they are there to stop you. If they don't, or can't, they are no good to you, but you must give them a chance.

(b) Conversely, do not get into the situation where everything you do is queried. There are often several ways of approaching a situation and you do not want to be explaining all day long why you chose a particular course.

(c) Whatever style you adopt, your managers and staff will subconsciously start to imitate it. I am by nature fairly choice with my language, and one day in the '60s I realized I had a shop full of extremely beautiful sales girls all effing and blinding their heads off. I said to the manageress that this didn't look too good to the customers, and we really should cut it out. 'I've already ****** warned them' she replied. These things are easy to start but stopping them can be a problem.

(d) Promotion is an area which can cause great unrest, unhappiness and therefore loss of efficiency among the staff. They can understand the introduction of specialists, accountants and production experts, but as you grow the staff that are the fundamentals – salespeople, line workers and so on – expect to grow with you. The problem is that they all expect to grow automatically at the same time, particularly those that started with you. Unfortunately, even if you had jobs for them and could afford it, the mere fact that they have been with you since you started and are extremely good at what they do does not qualify them for anything else. If you are lucky you will have employed some natural leaders along the way. I believe that whatever the disruption you should always, when possible, promote from within, otherwise you just lose the good ones, but be aware of the problems that you are creating.

The Management Team

You finally have a little cadre around you. Some you personally like more than others, some you may like very much indeed, but one thing is certain – they will not all like each other, and it is your job to make them into an effective unit. Firstly this means that you have to treat them all equally and evenly, and make them try to see things from each others' point of view, which ultimately must be your own – if it isn't you had better change the team.

Who will comprise this team? Given the fact that you are the average sort of trading company, you are going to have sales, production and accounting functions whether you are making the product yourself or subcontracting or buying it in ready-made. As soon as you start hiring a few people it is as well to have a personnel-type manager also, even if it justifies only part of that person's duties. So your basic team is most likely four people. Their individual standing within the team is likely to be as follows:

(a) Your accounts person will be loathed by everyone. He or she is probably a newcomer and is looked on by the rest as a direct infringement of their civil liberties – the right to spend your money – and as a cross between Scrooge and the Gestapo. You probably share their same opinion, for accountants are forever the bearers of bad news. You had better get over this blockage though, because this is where you are going to get your facts from, and without facts you are lost.

(b) Sales and Production will at least be united in dislike of accounts, but otherwise there's a running battle between them. Sales will always be taking orders for exactly the things that are causing Production problems, and Production will be ruining customer relationships by late/faulty delivery. Never mind, this argument will go on for ever, and as long as you keep it within bounds it is reasonably healthy.

(c) The outsider in this group is Personnel. If they are any good they will have a foot in both camps, 'management' and 'the rest'. At your meetings, because they count as 'management' occasions, they will tend to favour their role as defender of the masses and as such will be a pain in the neck to everybody. Let them have their say. Firstly it will make them and therefore the staff feel important and considered. Secondly, although you may think that the last thing you need to know while discussing perhaps the introduction of a new product that will break you if it fails, is that the new shift system involved will upset Sharon and Darren in clicking, picking or packing, in fact any alteration to established routines is going to cause discontent somewhere, and at a

57

later stage it could be critical, so you had better be aware of where the trouble is coming from and take steps to remove the cause before it happens. Your P.O. can at least make you aware that all is not well below before the mutiny happens. Again though, they are usually the bearer of bad news, and there is a great temptation to shut them out of your life.

Anyway, whatever your sort of business, at a certain moment your managers are going to be something like the above and, having hired them at great cost, you then must learn another very hard lesson, which is that you must let them get on with it. That does not mean that you can go and lie on a beach, but your role has changed. You hired them to have authority so you must let them run. This means that your relationship with the rest of the staff must change. They may be used to pouring out their troubles to you down at the boozer, or wandering into your office to give you a cream bun, but this has to stop. They must not think that you have abandoned them, but on the other hand they must be brought to realize that in the event of disagreement you will support the manager, at least in public. You may take him or her to pieces in private, but in public you *must* present a solid front. Far better to avoid these situations entirely, but if you are trapped, remember that the moment you have let the manager down in front of the staff you have in that instant undermined the entire structure that you have been trying to build, and you are in a mess that would make Houdini scratch his head.

The Union

As owner/manager of a small to medium business you tend to assume a certain amount of staff loyalty, and as long as nothing 'sudden' happens you are probably alright. By 'sudden' I mean an expansion, unpopular promotions from within, a change of direction or the introduction of managers or systems that disturb the status quo. Like a flock of sheep, the heads come up and everyone starts milling around wondering what is up. There need not be a specific or justifiable reason for this, the flock is threatened and they go into a defensive huddle, and this is typically when the spectre of the Union starts to shimmer over the horizon.

Being smugly secure in your abilities of benevolent leadership and man-management your first reaction is personal insult and outrage. You summon your managers, demanding to have the names of the ring leaders, and babble of instant dismissal, teaching them a lesson and whatever else takes your fancy. Your managers are probably as bewildered and hurt as you are, and rush out to do your bidding. You have just turned a serious blow to your ego into a potential chain reaction that could ruin you. What you must grasp is that unions exist and that your staff have every right to join one, irrespective of the circumstances.

Withdraw your managers from the front line of this particular battle. Their further involvement can only damage their standing once things settle down. They must go about their business as best they can, but they must *not* cause sparks. This one is down to you.

You will certainly be quickly contacted by the Area Officers of the Union. See them at once. Anything less and you are joining the King Canute persuasion. They will by this time have signed up a nucleus of membership in your business, who will most likely be the main agitators, and your first task is to ensure that they – the Union – actually have their new members under control. To do this you must give them something positive to relay back from their first meeting, otherwise anarchy prevails and this is a far more serious problem.

With any luck you and the Union are already starting to take the heat out of the situation. Then comes a period of negotiation, a deal is signed, and a committee of workers is elected. The moment they are elected, have a formal meeting with them to establish their standing in the eyes of their members and to relax them in their new importance. Treat them like gold dust. They can be the strongest management tool in your repertoire.

A good relationship with your union gives you a direct link, around the management structure to the darkest cavities of your business. Do not confuse what I am saying with weakness. The Union does not want you to be weak. They want their jobs, more so today than ever before. The vast majority of unions simply want to be acknowledged; when times are bad they will be your biggest support, if things are good they will want more money. If you can afford it, why not?

Dismissal

To ask someone to leave your employment is probably the closest you are ever going to be to playing God. If you have any feelings at all, and you won't last long if you don't, this is the time when you wonder why you ever started.

I'm not talking about sacking. I have sacked people for rape, prostitution, drug peddling, theft and mugging customers without a blink. It's straight and clear cut, no problems. Don't think twice about it. I mean the situation where you or your company have employed someone who is working away happily – maybe too happily – and you have tried everything you can think of to make them improve, without result. There's no other job you can possibly think of where they will work out, and that's when you start to feel sick.

Basically the fault is yours – you should never have hired them, and you are going to give them an enormous psychological jolt whichever way you wrap it up. However useless they are to you, they may be a treasure to someone else, as long as you do not destroy their self-confidence to the point where they no longer are able to give of their best.

Believe me, I know. I was once kicked out, for which I still believe were for the wrong reasons. That was 29 years ago, and if I met the man that engineered it today I would still wish to do him damage. Before I worked for myself, which was several years after that trauma, I was an employee like any one else – I was overlooked and disappointed, I was elevated and surprised, but I was handled fairly by proper managers and never felt resentment. Maybe I was lucky. I didn't think so – I was with the right people.

The big buzz-word in today's vernacular is 'personality clash'. You find two or more people on the payroll, sex or sexes unimportant, stark naked on the floor of your office, with several empty bottles of your drink rolling around. You kick them out and throw their clothes after them and the next morning they are ringing up to find out why their cards and personal belongings were delivered to their house by messenger at first light. 'Was it a personality clash?' they say.

In this sort of situation the only rules that you, the Boss, can afford to abide by are:

(a) If they have to go, make it as nice as you can in the circumstances.

(b) Get them off the premises at once. Feet must not touch the ground. The effect on the rest of the work-force of maudlin old mates, who within two seconds of being fired can manage to find and drink a half pint of the strong stuff, can cost you a serious disruption. Usually the staff have known what was going on long before you did, and would think the worst of you if you had not spotted it, or probably think you a fool for not seeing it sooner. As long as you do it properly and cleanly, everyone feels better, and works harder.

I hate to say it, but the odd judicious firing is perhaps your most effective way of showing everyone, management and staff alike, who is the Boss. Use this power rarely, but use it.

From the days when we had Biba, we must have hired and fired hundreds and hundreds of people, and we tried to be fair and proper. Almost wherever we go today somebody comes up and says, 'I used to work for you', and we cringe – what happened? We have met people in big jobs in big companies who have gone white at the sight of us and get us in a corner and say, 'you won't tell them that you sacked me?' and the answer is, 'Don't be stupid – I can't even remember'. More worrying is in restaurants, when the manager says, 'I used to work for you'. This is much more tense at the moment, because if you have others with you it is impossible to walk away with any dignity.

So now we always put the direct question, 'Did we sack you?' and they laugh and say, 'Of course you did' or, 'No you didn't'. Then they start delivering the free champagne. So the system works – if we have to do it, we do it right, and so must you. I am telling you the good bits, though. I can think of one person who is still padding the streets looking for me. . .

If reading all this makes you think that you can evolve a pre-set pattern for dealing with these unfortunate incidents, you are wrong. After we lost Biba we owned a company in São Paulo, Brazil. One of our production cutters was a man from Bolivia called Mr Willie. He was a nice man, father of a family and in his prime. His problem was that he did not cut very well. If he was cutting, say 500 garments, he would cough or blink or drop his cigarette and suddenly you were minus 500 left sleeves with no extra fabric to replace them. He was a menace. He had to go. This is an even bigger decision in Brazil than it is in the UK because there is almost no work around and machismo is a pride born of desperation that one must preserve.

So here am I building myself up to dismiss Mr Willie and there he is sitting in front of my desk. Sullen face, eyes impassive above high fleshy cheekbones. The dialogue, such as it was, ran roughly as follows:

I: We have some problems here.
            (N.B. The Fitz-Simon attack – always involve the other party in something that is bigger than both of us, cf. cash flow etc.)
WILLIE: Si, Mr Fitz.
I: This company has problems through loss of fabric.
WILLIE: Si, Mr Fitz.
I: . . . and many of the problems are caused by people not paying attention and woosh many mangas [sleeves] are gone for ever.
WILLIE: Si, Mr Fitz.
I: Mr Willie, therefore I cannot give you any more employment.
WILLIE: Mr Fitz I am going to kill you.

Here he takes out an enormous knife from behind his neck and places it against my throat, and nicks it a bit. By the wetness on my shoulder I can sense that this shirt is a no go for the cleaners.

Normally on these occasions, one should lean back and talk about the finer things – what he really wanted from life, his wife's needs, his aspirations for his children and anything else that might slow things up – but this was not what we had going for us at all. His eyes had become yellow slits, I felt mine popping out of my face. If I had cleared my throat I would have been looking for my tonsils on the floor.

My other disadvantage was that under pressure, I was thinking in English. Willie had never even heard of England. He was thinking in Spanish and speaking Portuguese.

The tableau vivant went on for several eons. Willie had made his move. It was up to me.

'Mr Willie.'

'Si, Mr Fitz.'

'I have good news for you. A mistake has been made – you have your job back.'

The slit eyes become round and full of tears, the knife is gone. I am being kissed on both cheeks, embraced and applauded as a 'real man'. As Willie leaves he meets Barbara coming in. More loud kissing, tears and embraces, 'Dona Barbara, thank you, thank you – I have my job back' etc. Barbara says, 'What went wrong?' By now I am using the rest of the shirt to hold back the blood.

Willie never made a mistake again, to my knowledge, nor did he ever capitalize on our little conversation. It would be nice to have him working here in England – but somehow I don't think he would fit in.

However smart you think you are when you really get down to it, one on one with real people, you never know. Don't worry if things go wrong – maybe you'll learn something.

6

Professional Advisers

Accountants

However bright you think you are, there are certain legal necessities in the running of a business that you are unable to do for yourself. At the end of each year you are going to need a properly qualified accountant, from outside your own business, to certify your financial state to the Income Tax authorities. Other financial paperwork also accumulates rapidly. Throughout the year there is information that you must supply to the Customs & Excise to whom you pay VAT, and the Department of Health & Social Security will be bombarding you with forms that need completing. If you have employees, someone has to calculate the deductions from their pay cheques, invoices start arriving and very quickly your workplace is full of bits of paper that need to be kept under control in a manner that will comply with the law. You simply do not have the time or energy to waste doing these things yourself. You should be so totally preoccupied with success or survival that all these relatively unimportant bits of paper go rapidly to the bottom of several piles, until one day someone has to spend time and your money sorting it all out. So the sooner you get everything properly organized the less trouble you will have in the future.

You have to run a fairly large company to justify the salary of a full-time, qualified accountant of your own, so it is usual to employ an outside specialist to handle all this for you. But what sort of accountant are you going to use? How are you going to find one and how will you know if they are right for you? This will be your first contact with 'professionals', and although they will never make you rich they can most certainly break you, both financially and mentally. If you fall in with the wrong person you will certainly find yourself in deep trouble.

Apart from bank managers and artist's agents I have heard more bad language used about accountants than any other sector of the business community. Obviously, they cannot all be bad all the time, or they would be out of work themselves. The fact is that you, particularly at the start of your career, probably expect much too much from your accountant in the way of general advice and expertise, and they, being human, are only too pleased to act as a professional guru, without having any aptitude at all for the stab and grab of commercial life. Your average accountant has spent several years slogging through some fairly straightforward exams to become a member of a profession that is basically concerned with the recording of commercial fact rather than initiative or wheeling and dealing. When they have a go at this for themselves they frequently get into the most awful mess, which is all right as long as you are not part of it.

Choosing an accountant

Here are some basic things to consider before you make your choice.

First, what size of company should you go to? As a small outfit, you will probably not be best suited to or welcomed by the giants, as they are simply not geared up for you, nor you for them, but that does not mean that you have to go to a back street genius. No one wants to be in a back street for ever, so the fact that they are there means either that they, like you, are starting out or that they have failed to progress. In the first case, let them practise on someone else. In the second, the answer is obvious – stay away.

There are, however, thousands, if not tens of thousands, of middle-sized concerns who can do the basic jobs you need, who have reasonable addresses and fancy letterheads, and who can present your case to the bank or tax-man on decent stationery and generally add a touch of veracity to your humble offerings. Most important is the person within the firm who deals with you and your business. They will have access to your innermost financial secrets, which is fine if things are going well but this is not always the case. Because the worse you do, the more you will need to be in touch, it is essential that you have roughly the same commercial philosophy and basic attitude.

You should always remember, when dealing with accountants, that figures in themselves mean very little – it's the interpretation of them that counts. I had one accountant whose sole interest appeared to be to make me go bust as fast as he could. On the first set of figures he produced he declared that he 'saw much money coming in and much money going out' and that in future he wanted payment in advance. I took the same figures to another firm who said I was doing nicely and showing a profit at an early stage and I was able to relax and get about my business.

More dangerous, though, is the adviser who tells you that you are doing well. Believe me, this is never the case. You may be doing well enough at the time, you may even have a great future, but the moment that you really believe that all is fine is the moment you are in trouble. You may be doing better, which is nice to know, but if you cannot see the possibility of disaster on the horizon, then you should forget almost everything else and start looking. You may not be able to avert all hazards but you can certainly be ready.

I have been through more accountants than most, so I will give you some case histories, and even if they do not apply to you now bear them in mind.

I inherited my first accountant from my wife, who was a substantial earner in her own right. He was deeply suspicious of my motives, and was convinced that I had married strictly for money. We decided to start a part-time business together, selling my wife's designs by post. In six months it did not work and money was going out – I think we were about £100 to the bad, which even in 1964 was not a fortune. I received a call at work from the accountant, calling me all kinds of names for my financial recklessness. The way he put it really shook me, and I found myself agreeing with him that we should wind up the business. There was, however, one last editorial appearing in the Daily Mirror, which was too late to stop. We resolved that it would be the last one. As it happened we hit the jackpot – we sold 26,000 dresses in about two weeks, managed to get them made and delivered and had only 90 sent back, which we promptly delivered elsewhere. Our lives changed overnight, we were rocketed out of the norm and into a world where we were responsible for our own destiny. If we had not struck lucky then we would have listened to the voice of comfortable reason and maybe wound up as spectators rather than doers, and would never have known how close we were. When you start you do not need the hand of reason on your shoulder – it will always be pulling you back. You need energy and confidence to blast clear of the wet blankets of the faint-hearted and get on with whatever you are doing.

A few months later we had a shop. We did not know too much about shopkeeping or business in general but we kept making things and people kept buying them. It did not mean that we had any money, however. The more we sold, the larger stock we had to carry and in cash flow terms things were tight. My accountant, to whom I was now a hero, put all our administration on an automatic accounting machine that operated from his office – this was in a pre-computer age. Every week, beautifully typed cheques would arrive, ready for my signature. As there was no money in the bank, there was little point in signing the vast majority of them, so I put them in a drawer, and if a creditor became particularly abusive, I would pull one out and pay him. After three or four months my man came to visit, congratulating us on our success and himself on his system. I showed him the drawer full of cheques, and I though he was going to pass out – he simply could not believe it. 'What do you mean, you didn't sign them? I have produced them, they are due, everything is in order. You must pay them *now*!'

He could not conceive that just because he was correct in theory things did not work that way in real life.

We struggled on together for several more months, but it was no good. To him, it was my over-riding duty to pay the cheques churned out by his beautiful machine. He would come to my office, dash to the drawer and sit there brooding on the enormity of my sins. In the end I moved most of them to another drawer without his knowledge, which seemed to please him. We parted company, and he has since worked for friends of mine with a very large business who think him marvellous, which goes to show, though what I couldn't tell you.

By this time we were starting to become quite big, and I turned to one of the largest accounting firms in the world. They put in consultants, did audits and projections, installed systems and management. They cost a fortune but in the organizational sense they were worth it, as I still use bits of their basic system 20 years later, but they too nearly cooked me in another way.

About that time our ambitions and financial capacity parted company quickly and dramatically, and I was running round the

City, and anywhere else I could smell a few hundred thousand pounds, trying to put things right. Negotiations culminated in a large meeting of potential investors at a certain large and respectable bank. I had already distributed in advance the reams of paper produced by my consultants, which showed a reasonably rosy future if the money came in. I had the head consultant with me to answer any questions and generally be in support. I had told him before the meeting, 'You've done all the figures, don't say anything fancy, just tell the truth'. When the Chairman asked him for his comments he stood up and sold me and the work I had paid him to do straight down the river. He said that it was all based on conjecture, that he didn't believe what I had been telling him etc., etc. The Chairman thanked him and said he could leave. I sat there looking at my potential investors and they sat looking at me, and I must have looked sick. Finally, one of them said, 'Have you paid that guy?' I said 'Yes', feeling sicker by the minute. Someone else said 'We don't need *him* again', I think that they were all so annoyed at this betrayal that it swung the deal for me – everybody felt that they had been let down.

On another occasion a Brazilian accountant negotiated a big loan for me with a director of one of the banks. I went to collect him on the way to sign the documents, to learn that both he and the banker were in the local slammer. If I had signed up I would have been in there with them

During a big leap forward in early days, and a move to a larger shop, an English accountant worked out that I would go out of business for the lack of £2,000. This is very depressing news, particularly when your entire energies are devoted to the absolute necessity of opening the doors on time. We met with two what we might call 'fringe' bankers, both in crocodile Gucci shoes, who said that for 25% of the company we could have the money and please sign here. We said no, and the accountant went ape in the street outside. We made our goodbyes and went back to work. The shop opened next day and we took £2,000 in the first morning. End of problem, but there was the accountant with his tongue hanging out asking if he could physically count the money – he had never seen £2,000 in readies before. End of another accountant.

When I told the poor man who is now handling our affairs that

I was going to write something about his profession, and that my advice was not to pay their bills, he thought that was extremely funny, which considering the state of my account with him was just as well – but it has taken me over 20 years to find such a person. I hope he is still acting on our behalf, if he ever reads this.

Lawyers and the Law

Most of the yardsticks in the selection of your accountant apply equally well to your solicitor – size of firm and personal compatibility should go without saying. The difference, however, in your dealings with your lawyers is that, apart from the odd will and property transaction, you will only need them when you are in trouble, and the odds are that you will be in a great hurry and in a state of some excitement. Therefore, to me the major factor in making your choice is, can you get hold of them when you want them rather than when they have time for you?

The economics of a lawyers office are such that they are all of them on a fairly tight margin and it is only the very big concerns who are able to run to knowledgeable assistants who can help you if the Partner is doing something else, and they are usually very expensive. There is nothing more nerve-racking than to sit waiting for a return call to discover just how much of a mess you are in. I was in such a situation about a year ago and when I finally made contact and explained my plight the reply came, 'Oh that's nothing, I have a man on the other line who has the bailiffs in', which was of little help or encouragement. On the other hand he was a good solicitor, as many in the profession desert the ship long before this unhappy moment, and if you are in real trouble will insist on payment in advance and other strictures that they know full well you cannot manage. It is therefore best that they should never know the true extent of your finances. Like banks, never let them deal with both your business and private affairs, so that the myth that there is always money in the other pocket can be preserved and used to prevent this type of unpleasantness.

Lawyers are no different from other professional people and can best be compared to doctors. The average solicitor is the General Practitioner, who should quickly pass you on to the expert if your case is anything but standard, but because in theory all solicitors are equal, and want the work, this does not happen, so it is up to you to find the expert in your type of business. The fact that a firm has represented your family for three generations is, if anything, a minus. What you really need is a good honest shyster (whatever that is) who will pull every trick going on your behalf. One of the best people who ever acted for me actually started off on the other side. My own advisers kept muttering and telling me what a rogue he was and how he should be disbarred. After he had taken me to the cleaners I rang him up and off we went with a very satisfactory run of success.

Remember, though, that however in the mire you feel you are, the law is there to protect you as well as the other party and if your adviser knows how to use it you will be amazed at what is going for you. The facts of commercial life are such that no entrepreneur gives the slightest thought to the law in his day-to-day transactions. Instructions and orders are placed by telephone, deals are done in a moment and if something goes wrong, and matters come to court, both sides are very often on legally sticky ground, whereas in the United States you can hardly say 'Good Morning' without your attorney beside you. Thankfully we are not in this situation in the UK or even, in my experience, anywhere else in the world – except possibly Japan. Here, it is normally only the rogues or incompetents who start showering you with legal letters at the drop of a hat. The average person simply has neither time or inclination for such activity, except as a last resort, and even then you should be careful. At the time of writing I myself have never sued anyone and I hope I never will be so stupid as to put myself in a situation where I have no other option.

However, you may well find that people insist on suing you, which means they want your money. There are three normal reasons why they have taken such a course.

(a) You owe them and cannot pay.
(b) You owe them and you do not want to pay, because they have done something to your detriment.
(c) You have let them down in a way that has cost them money and they want it back.

For amounts under £5,000 the summons will come from the

County Court. For bigger sums the writ will probably arrive from the High Court, and your response must be geared accordingly, particularly in situation (a) – lack of funds. Here, as we will examine in another section, your need is one of time. A County Court writ can give you a healthy breathing space, which may run into months if you handle it correctly. Here you should not involve your lawyer in the first instance. At the back of the writ is a form where you can enter your defence. Use your best handwriting (no typewriter) and tell the court why you think that you should not have to pay. Better still, elaborate on how hard done by you have been and give a rough assessment of the damage that you have suffered. Enclose as much supporting paper as you can find, even internal memos or personal notes, and if credibly possible arrive at a loss to yourself or your company, caused by the activities of the Plaintiff, that is very much higher than the amount that he is after from you.

This, if well done, has three immediate effects:
(a) Your persecutor will be unable to achieve the summary justice that he expects and is now involved in legal fees of his own.
(b) You will be asked to attend a preliminary hearing at the Court, which can give you anything up to two months' leeway.
(c) The person chasing you, in the full flower of self righteousness, suddenly finds that if he loses he is going to have to pay you much more than he is actually trying to get. This is going to make him very angry, thereby muddling his thinking and, if he has any sense, it will slow him up. You will, in the normal process of these things, receive a letter from his lawyer, asking to be put in touch with yours, and if your side knows what they are doing it will run and run.

A High Court writ is something else again. Your lawyer has to respond, and although your aggression should not be any less, your facts have to be extremely well based and generally your opportunities for prevarication are limited. This is when your advisors earn their money, so run to them as fast as you can.

The fact that you are now in the highly experienced hands of the professional person of your choice is no reason to relax. Your

71

fate is now down to someone to whom you are just another punter with a problem, who has financial problems of his own and who probably makes 90% of his or her income in servicing one or two major clients that he or she cannot afford to lose, so you are entitled to worry as much as you like. You will be dealt with in exactly the same way as you handle your own minor customers – at the last minute and then only if pushed. So your problem has suddenly changed. The obstacle is your own team, not the enemy. This is why you must have the personal empathy that I have mentioned. Without that you will always be at the end of the queue, and things will be negotiated on your behalf, at the very last minute, to which you would never, or more likely, could never have agreed.

I have had triumphant voices ringing me of an evening to tell me that a case that I had thought to be months from any activity has now been resolved. 'They've given in, Fitz – I really pushed them. They've accepted £12,000 and not £14,000. All you have to do is get a bank draft round to their office by 12.00 tomorrow and that's the end of it.' As you are at the time £10,000 over at the bank and busy trying to stretch it to £15,000 you are not too well pleased. You know that at about 12.20 you will start to receive outraged calls from your own lawyer followed rapidly by heavy bills and suddenly you are the baddie, and you are in worse trouble than before. I hate to say it, but it is all your fault, because you have lost control of your own destiny, and inevitably you will suffer.

Publicity & Public Relations

Barbara and I have always agreed that as soon as you believe your own publicity, you are on the slippery slope to your downfall. I have seen this happen, and you must be most careful about how you approach the whole subject. Publicity for your company can be an enormous factor in your success but it can also be a complete waste of money and time, plus a means of self delusion that, taken together, can have very negative effects.

There are two types of publicity – one that you know you have paid for, which is called Advertising, and the other which you think has cost you nothing, which is called Editorial.

Advertising

You decide that what you are pedalling will benefit if it is known to a wider audience. Depending on the nature and geographical distribution of your product you have the choice of anything from the Yellow Pages, via your local newspaper to a publication with national coverage, and there are many fine advertising agencies to help you on your way. As with Lawyers and Accountants the problem is do you need to use an agency, and if so, which should you choose?

If you are about to invest £10 in a classified ad in your local newspaper, you obviously don't need a professional, and none of them will look at you anyway. Do not denigrate their art, however, because there are certain unsaid rules and traps that they know all about and you do not, and the fact that you doubled your sales last week does not make you an expert in the promotion of your business over the long term. If you are about to spend any amount of money that is important to you, it is essential that you have professional advice, or you will be throwing it away.

There is one nicety to be aware of here. You know your product – you may even have grown to love it, but the Agency people see it in a very different context, and if you are to take the next great step forward you should listen to them, and examine their motives very carefully. What they are trying to do is sell you their ideas, or 'campaign' as they insist on calling it, and if they fail they will be out of pocket, so they are more concerned with your reaction than that of the punters you are trying to reach. Therefore the less you know them personally, the better, or they will do an ad that they think you want to see, rather than one that might work. That is why most large companies employ an advertising manager – and possibly even a department – to keep the personal influences at bay. When you stumble into your first meeting with your agency, particularly after they have lunched you, you will have no idea at all what is happening, and will lurch away into the sunset with the glowing thought that you have met some very nice young people, all of them dedicated to your further success. That's what their job is all about. I know – I once was one of them.

In reality, there are very few instances where even the right ad, in the right place ever made much difference to the success of a product. It may have helped, but it can only, the way things are, have been marginal to its ultimate fate.

Editorial Publicity & Public Relations People

Editorial publicity is an article or a mention in a publication for which you have not directly paid. At the local level, you may know someone who is married to the person writing the What's New column in the weekly newspaper, who may give you a mention for old times sake and peace and quiet, and it could be very important for you indeed. Even if your friendship is more than close, however, there is a limit to the number of free plugs that can be justified, so you come back to advertising. You will find that the fact that you are spending your own money with the paper will encourage them to increase the strike rate of your 'mentions', and so it goes on. That is really all you can do.

If you are aiming for national distribution and have no connection with the media at that level, you are going to find that you need a Public Relations Organization to make any impression at all, and this is where the money can disappear faster than you could ever believe.

Most PRs are hacks who make their living by who they know, and they can be far more expensive than you might think at first glance. Minicabs delivering samples, little lunches and deals on the side can run you into very large numbers indeed. I fell right into it when we were launching our cosmetic company. A delightful PR lady sold me the idea of 'sponsoring' photographic sessions. The theory is that if you pay, the make-up artist will use your product and you will be credited in the feature. What I did not know was that, a) these people have hyped themselves to the £150 per day level, and b) irrespective of whose product is used, he who pays gets the credit. Of course, the large companies had rumbled this long ago, but as I was a newcomer and therefore green, it was open season on S.C.Fitz-Simon. I was inundated by invoices from people I had never heard of, for photographs I never did see, and that probably were never used, or if they were some other sucker must have paid up.

It proved very hard to stop. Agents were blocking my telephone, demanding payment for 'poor little Eva' who had worked her tiny fingers off on my behalf last month. I looked at about £5,000 of invoices on my desk and tore them up, and the next whizz-kid that called received the short end of it. This went on for several weeks, until one particularly virulent harridan informed me that my name was mud and that no one would ever work for me again, which cheered me up considerably.

If you do have your product featured heavily in the national press, do not expect too much, or indeed anything at all. Its pulling power is as fickle and unpredictable as that of mail order, and the response can very easily be near nil. Although an editorial was the making of us, this was an exception – we had found a loophole in the market that lasted for roughly five months, during which time our sales by post were phenomenal. Then the gates slammed shut, and, I believe, never reopened.

What is important is that your publicity is steady and consistent. How many ads do you remember from last night's TV? On the Chinese water torture principal, you have to keep dripping away in order to be noticed.

Trade Mark Agents

If you have a branded product that you think will have a big market, not only at home but in other countries, you are rightly going to feel the need to protect its name so that it cannot be used by others, who may even prevent you from using it yourself. To do this you have to employ a specialist Trade Marks agent and the sooner you go and see one the better, if only to give yourself an idea of what is involved and how much it will cost. The specialist agent has a network of local contacts throughout the world, so you are in fact hiring the services of a resident expert in each country in which you want to be protected.

Your product or range will fall into one or more categories that have been internationally agreed. These categories are loose groupings of products which are often only vaguely similar, and this is where both complications and expenses start to increase. Anyone who has a product in the same category, however dissimilar it may in fact be, and with a name that can conceivably be confused with yours, can and most likely will enter an objection, and then the fun begins. If everything goes smoothly the cost of registering your name in one category in one country is around £400, and you will have other costs spread over the years to maintain that status. Unless you are most careful it can be a very expensive game.

Early on in the life of your business you may well be so concerned with what is happening on your own front doorstep that you leave the rest of the world to look after itself. You probably will not realize, unless you are exceptionally far-sighted or conceited, just how big you are going to become. Certainly we had no such idea when we started Biba, but some crafty fellow in Paris was way ahead of us, as we found out a couple of years later when we wanted to open a shop there only to find that we could not use our own name. We were lucky that it only happened that once. Your agent will be able to advise, but they will have their own idea of priorities, so be very sure what you are letting yourself in for before you start them rolling.

7

Big Problems

A Big Problem is one that will put you out of business if you do
not solve it very quickly indeed. It may in fact not be one problem
but a series of small ones that together have the same effect. At
some stage in their life these problems were either remote
possibilities that could be discounted, or so distant that their
existence was completely ignored until there they are, leering
at you wherever you look, threatening the existence of all that
you have built or hope to build. They are threatening not only
your business but your entire life and that of your family. You
quite possibly have everything you own on the line, right back to
your house and your and your wife's personal guarantees on the
bank overdraft. In fact, however 'limited' your company may
legally be, your own personal liability is such that you could
never in a month of Sundays pay off what you owe on even a good
employee's salary were you forced to cease trading.

The prospect is really awful. It is no good your advisers asking
you how you arrived at such a mess and giving you homilies on
business prudence, no good moaning at what might have been –
you are in the mess now and the sooner you face up to it, the
greater the chance of survival. You must do something. The
problem is not going to disappear. It will get bigger and bigger
until it is too late, and it has brought you down. If ever you
personally are going to earn you money, it is now. This is what
really sorts out the winners from the losers.

The first thing to realize is that you are not unique in this
miserable situation. Ask any successful business person if they
have ever been nearly bust and if they are honest they will say
yes. If they are extremely honest they will say, 'Several times'.
Such is the nature of business, and if you do not like it you should
never have started.

Your biggest danger is that your thought-processes will
become so clogged by the enormity of what is about to happen
that you cease to function. You must force yourself to take a cold
and pragmatic view of the situation. You are fighting for your

existence and nothing at all must interfere with what you have to do. A typical first reaction is to busy yourself with the day to day running of the business. You take triumph in the resuscitation of an account long dead. You worry that the books are not quite up-to-date, you busy yourself in the petty cash and your secretary's personal problems. You travel miles to take an order from a customer for whom you would not give two monkey's in normal times. You are 'doing things'. A runaway bus is upon you and you are busy changing your underwear so that you will look good in the mortuary – *stop it*. Concentrate on the matter in hand – survival.

First you must define your problem. Apart from your own resolution, this is the most important part. If you do not get this right then everything else you do will fail. You probably think that you know why it happened but you must be really sure that you are right. You may have to go over this in great detail with a large number of people before you are through.

Second, the visible result of your problems is always that you owe substantially more money than you can pay in a reasonable period of time. Make sure that you know exactly how much and to whom every last penny is due. Not just those who are shouting loudest, or who are owed the larger amounts, but everyone down to the shop on the corner. Include your personal finances because in this situation they have the same standing, as far as you are concerned, as those of your company. List everything, and categorize them by when you feel you will have to pay them – not when they want to be paid, or might even insist on being paid, but when they will get around to the writing of writs, or the repossession of your house. Pay most particular attention to your trade suppliers. Do you have all you need to support your current orders, or will you have to pay them before they deliver essential items?

Then make yourself a simple cash flow, doing the outgoings first, so that you are looking at the best position you think that you can engineer. Now treat your debtors in exactly the same way. Will any of them pay you early if you offer a discount? If your bank is pressing, will any give you cash for a bigger discount? Will any be induced to buy more from you for an even greater discount etc., etc. Enter this into your cash flow, add orders and payments that you can pessimistically expect over the critical period, and at least you have what you feel to be a realistic assessment of the true scale of the problem. It may not make you any happier, but you are facing it and have something to work against.

You will probably find, if you have brought yourself to undertake this calculation, that you owe more than you thought but that you are not going to be hauled off to Carey Street this week, or with any luck, even this month. So you should have time to make your moves, whatever they may be. They obviously depend on why you are in trouble in the first place and whether or not, in the foreseeable course of events, you will be able to trade your way out of it.

In the UK a very large percentage of companies are under-capitalized and rely on pure cash flow to see them through. This means that if something goes wrong and the sales or work do not materialize as expected, short term financial problems appear almost at once. Many companies that can scratch up a reasonable set of figures at the end of the year are living on a knife edge, and in the nature of their business always will be, unless they can persuade someone to put in some capital. At the same time, their proprietors are naturally reluctant to share their baby and illusory independance with others. I fully sympathize with that attitude. On the other hand it is better to have x% of something than no percent of nothing, or at best 100% of a company that will lurch from crisis to crisis until the early death of its owner. It all depends on who is your partner.

I am saying this to cheer you up if you have to face the abhorrent idea that you are not going to trade out of your present embarrassment and that the introduction of money from outside is essential if you are to survive. Believe me, it is much more fun running a company that has money in the bank, pays its bills on time and can make decisions based on hard cash in the hand, than a life-time scratching round trying to pay the wages. So do not be too shocked or depressed if you come to the reluctant conclusion that this is the only way out. In the state you are in, your problem is not should you go for investment but how on earth are you going to get it?

At this stage you will start to become very busy indeed. Your first worry is to make all the events, the delays and prepayments in your emergency cash flow actually happen. It is very demeaning to have to ring people to explain that you have a little problem that will take a few weeks to sort out, when for the past year you have been cursing them for slip-shod work and generally making a pig of yourself. As you are undoubtedly late with your payment as well, this will not be treated with much support and understanding, but if they are key suppliers you must take them along with you, for if you do get out of the mire you are going to need them. As you will have noticed in yourself, I hope, people become very funny where cash is concerned, so that although you should avoid telling direct and detectable lies you should stretch the truth into whichever shape you think will have the most appeal.

At the same time you should be preparing what is in effect a prospectus of your company that you can show to prospective punters. How you present this is a matter of extreme delicacy. At one end you cannot tell the whole sorry situation in one breath. 'If I do not get £50,000 by next week, I will be at the cleaners,' may be the nub of it, but as an invitation to a profitable partnership it clearly sets the wrong tone. Again, you must not tell lies or you may find yourself behind bars. Before your deal is over someone will wish to authenticate your figures, or at least make you and your fellow directors give a personal guarantee that they are correct. I know so many idiots who have fiddled a few noughts here and there that made no difference to the viability of their offer, and who have lost out completely because of this. It must be the vanity of the moment, for if things do not add up and generally make sense they will come apart, and that will be that. The first thing a prospective partner wants to know is, 'Can I trust the person I am doing business with?' and if they find you fiddling in the first five seconds, the answer is going to be 'No'.

Whatever your circumstances or type of business there are some basic common denominators that any potential investors are going to be looking at above all else.

The first one is you, your track record, present attitude and
   enthusiasm for the future.
Second is the contribution that they can make to the success of
   what will be a company that you jointly own.

Third, what can you do for their business. They have their own
problems.

Fourth, absolutely critical, do they like you, and other key
people that are in your company? They will want to spend time
with you. See you socially, meet your spouse etc. If things go
well, they are going to be with you for a long time, and you
with them. I have never known a person who has turned down
a catastrophe saving deal because they did not like the other
side. I have known plenty who said yes at the moment of
disaster, and have lived miserable lives ever since. At the time
your vision of the future is completely fogged by the facts of
the day. However, this rule is not infallible. We did a deal
once, in exactly these circumstances, and those that we liked
least when we signed became friends, and the rest we had to
unload as fast as we could.

In the meantime, while you are pumping yourself up with
thoughts of deals and rescues, 'White Knights' and other
fantasies, spending your days with accountants and contact men
and people in the City, reality is taking place at the office. Given
the fact that you have done your number on those creditors that
you know to be dangerous, i.e., those to whom you owe the most
money, or those whose produce you need at the moment, there
will still be many smaller amounts owed to suppliers that you
have not contacted. A person to whom you owe £10,000 is going
to be far more understanding when you tell him you need some
more time than one who is owed £100 – he cannot imagine a
situation where you do not have a spare £100 or even £1000, and
the truth is you probably do. It is very easy for even a small
company to owe over £10,000 in minor amounts, any one of
which you could pay tomorrow, but together they add up to a
formidable sum, enough to pay off your £10,000 man, who one
day will get terminal if you cannot cough up. The day you have to
pay him you will need that £10,000 in the bank, not £9,000,
because you paid the difference to Jack, the transport man, who
is a bit pushed that week.

Back in the office, your telephonist and whoever you have put
in charge of these things are talking to old Jack and his ilk all day
long and are wondering what is going on. Now you have a

dilemma. You cannot afford to be subjected to all this rubbish. Jack's feeble excuses as to why he needs his money are of absolutely no interest to you, but your company is sinking fast, and if you are not careful this will be transmitted outwards, to your detriment. If you are not careful you will have dozens of old Jacks besieging your place of work demanding payment, which drives morale even lower.

This is particularly depressing if you are in the service or creative areas, where your stock in trade is your employees, whom, as you are coming to the moment when their wages are beyond your means, you are going to have to start sacking. Be careful here though. The law being what it is you can find that the amount it costs to rid yourself of what you now regard as their stupid faces, grazing on whatever reserves you have left, is beyond your short-term ability to produce, so you can easily find yourself stuck with an overhead that you can afford neither to pay nor to chop.

As the pressure mounts and the work load drops (because that is probably the problem in the first place) your staff are going to become increasingly dissatisfied, and if you are not careful you will have an 'us and them' situation which, if allowed to go too far, can result in having them working against you. The rot can very quickly start from within, and although you cannot, in the light of the marvellous things that you are totally preoccupied in accomplishing, afford to get your head back in the sand of day-to-day inadequacies, remember what happened to Napoleon at Waterloo, when the Prussians came wandering in on his left flank and spoiled everything. However necessary it is for you to divorce yourself from day-to-day lunacies you must keep the overall perspective of what is happening and rally yourself and such troops as you may have to the next breach.

We will come back later to your deal and how it might proceed. One thing of which you can be certain is that it is not happening at the sort of pace that you wish. Those who are putting money into situations have a very different time scale from your own, and if you reveal the pressures upon you to their full extent either you will put them off it entirely, because being chancers themselves they will lose respect for you for having shown your hand, or they, being company men, will screw you into the ground and you will wind up with 20% of 'B' shares unfranchiseable until you have paid them back and made a million on top. This will give you a mill-stone mentality which defeats the entire purpose, but this is what company men do. Here you are again, back at the crumbling fort, trying to fight off the Indians, who by this point constitute anyone who makes contact, especially those knocking at the door. As you cannot pay them, all you can do is stave them off, while trying to preserve the goodwill of those that you will need for the future and gaining time away from the massed ranks of those who you never want to see again.

All this is very unpleasant, and quite contrary to your highly creative, individualistic and aggressive nature, but we must forget about you for a minute, and think about them, and try to categorize them and treat them accordingly. They will fall roughly into certain behaviour patterns.

The most tiresome are those who insist on visiting you, in the expectation that their plight, personality and persuasive powers will do the trick. These all want to speak to you personally and will spend all day disrupting your place of work unless they can see you. Some want to talk, some to collect, and some to thump you as well as walk away with the cash. Others send men to do it for them. The wear and tear on yourself from the constant bombardment from these people can seriously blunt your thrust. Much best if you are not there, particularly if one or more mobs arrive at the same time. The effort of playing all these assorted gentry off against each other, although in other circumstances quite amusing, is most debilitating at that moment and should be avoided. I once had an office with a loo straight off the reception area, which I visited at about 10.00 one morning. I was stuck there all day while platoons of would-be debt collectors came and left. Barbara had to bring me books and sandwiches every few hours to keep me sane. An ex-semi-associate of mine in a very hard business has an infallible cure for this type of visitor. He says 'What's your name?' and when the man tells him he replies, 'I thought so, there was a man with a gun around here looking for you yesterday.' End of interview. The important thing here is to avoid personal confrontation, because this can be nasty and can also limit your room for manoeuvring. Those who are particularly obnoxious you can ring the next day, using lines such as, 'I heard you sent a gorilla round to my place yesterday', (knowing full well that it was the M.D.) 'You do that again and I'll have my man break his ****** neck!'

The easy ones are those who keep ringing, to whom you are 'out' and send you plaintive and/or threatening letters. They are so pleased when you do speak to them that you get another two weeks' grace before they start the whole proceedings again. The weirdest form of debt collecting I ever encountered was in Brazil, where one man, who was in some ways a person of influence, would ring my office and announce that he would not leave his telephone until I rang. He would stay there half the night – we used to check it by calling him and putting the phone down, and there he sat, fuming and threatening. I would ring him the next day and tell him that I had been trying to talk to him all evening, but his phone had been cut off. As a joke it was marvellous, but as an exercise in conceit there must be something to be learnt by someone.

The one thing you must avoid is lack of eating money for you and your family. If you are worried about how you and yours personally are going to get through tomorrow, everything goes out of the window except your desperate need for a £50 note. At the first sign of trouble, make sure that you have enough hard cash under the mattress to see you through the foreseeable crisis period. You have to look after your own in these hard times, and hard luck on the others.

Now back to your deal. You have your figures, your prospectus, now you need someone to look at them, and hopefully to talk to. These things move in mysterious ways . . . I have been to lunch with the directors of several major banks in my time, both merchant and clearing, and come away with nothing but indigestion. I have met drunks in pubs who have put me in touch with the most amazing beneficial situations. There is nothing I can say to you that can relate to your own special situation and connection, except that, within reason, the bigger the money you are chasing, the more people of substance will listen. It is relatively easy to make a case for £100,000 but almost impossible for £10,000, but, whatever you need, make sure that you can justify what you are asking for. Remember that today's sucker may be tomorrow's partner, so treat everything on the assumption that the deal will go ahead. Commit yourself to it wholeheartedly and positively and you will carry others with you. The slightest doubt or climb-down on your basic premise and all is lost.

The men with money have no interest in your petty cash book and do not want to read pages of analysis of your present status or waffle about your aspirations. They see all that ten times a day. They are only interested in you, and what you will start to do for them as the ink dries on the paper, and therefore what you will be doing for yourself. So put your head down and go for the big time, because if you do not try it, you'll never know what it's like, and if you have read so far, you're not the person I hope you are if you don't give it a shot. An old multi-millionaire, who had spent his life in the rag trade, said to me as he drove me home in his extremely new Rolls Royce, 'Remember, you're never broke until you run out of money' – and he was right.

8

Out of Hours

Although I have tried to keep this book as non-sexist as I can, here I have to write as what I am, a male of hetero persuasion. If I try it any other way it will have no veracity. If you are a feminist, for him read her or vice versa.

Friends

As you start out on your own you will acquire two illusory assets which are probably strangers to you; one is financial independence, and therefore the assumption in the minds of others that you have riches, and the other is power. You can employ people, put business their way and generally have a potential for advancing the cause of your friends and ex-associates, which in their minds will be out of all proportion to your true situation.

Unless you are really insensitive, you will be aware of your new status immediately. For openers, your ex-business colleague becomes your extremely jealous old mate, and will offer you the services of his wife as your secretary, and anything else he can think of primarily in order to keep track of your progress and, subconsciously, to bring you back to a level that he understands.

He realizes that you have escaped from the fold, but he cannot fathom how. He is actually very upset indeed, as your sudden independence reflects in some oblique way on his own situation. His career, which may well have been far more successful than your own, has suddenly taken a psychological dive. Overnight you have entered a different work warp and your whole thinking and motivation are light years from his own – not necessarily better, but definitely different. You are playing in another league. He can see it, but you don't because you should be so concerned with what happens next that this aspect should never cross your mind.

If you persist with a relationship with someone who reacts like this, the snide remarks start coming in, followed by the quick tap-up for the short-term loan. If you are a cash-taking business you'll get 'Can you do a cheque on a Saturday, dated to the end of the month?' If you say yes he hates himself, and if you refuse he's not too fond of you either. If you move house or buy another car or anything that can be seen as a success symbol, even if you are living in a doss house at the time, this will go down as a direct insult to his own status and achievements, and somewhere along the line you are going to have a blood bath. So best sever the connection. All they are really doing is trying to drag you back to the same old cesspit, and the sooner you realize that you are not the jolly, carefree lad of yesterday, the less aggravation all round.

Another misconception on the part of your acquaintances is that they are doing you a favour by patronizing your wares, usually at a big discount. We were particularly vulnerable to this form of friendship because we owned a shop, but I know from talking to others that it applies right through the commercial spectrum. People would arrive with big hellos, normally at the end of the day, and start criticizing and trying on clothes and generally doing us a good turn. As the pile of objects that they wanted grew larger, Barbara and I would become correspondingly more depressed. What they bought, or their opinions, were of no interest to us at all. We would have gladly given them a £5 note to go away, but the charade had to be played out.

The moment of reckoning comes, and cheque-books are being waved around. 'How much is it did you say . . . ?', and in the end you give them a discount to get rid of them. If we had asked them to lend us their car, or let us stay in their house for a couple of days in exchange they would have thought us beyond the pale, but discounts don't count. The fact that we were actually giving them our money never entered their selfish heads. Quite soon we hardened up and another bunch of bosom buddies went down the drain. This is why film stars tend to stick with their own and millionaires have yachts, because as far as they are concerned that is the norm, and they don't want thousands of idiots trying to cash in on them. It applies all the way down the line, to wherever you happen to be.

Spouses

At least, you can elbow this sort of friend, but a far more immovable object is your family. In my case I was lucky, as my wife and I started our business together, as equals, and have stayed that way. Others are not so fortunate. There are few things more disruptive or undermining for your staff than to have a spouse who arrives like the Queen or King of the May and expects to be treated as such. I have seen whole factories stop while the spouse goes round greeting the workers, distributing largesse and kisses, and generally being a nuisance. Your spouse may be your partner in life and its finer elements, but in the context of your business he or she constitutes a menace that you must control at the earliest possible stage.

In any business, whatever size, the staff quickly establish a psychological ecology for their own survival. Even if it is only you and one other, gender is almost irrevelant – your relationship is going to develop in a way that you can both live with, and if it doesn't then drop it at once. As you grow bigger and involve more people, they are going to sort out a framework of relationships that more or less suits everybody. There are certain things that you can do to control this, mainly in the hiring, firing and promoting areas. You will never dominate it, but you should try. You should watch very carefully what is happening in the unofficial pecking order, for from it you will have some insight into your potential leaders and trouble-makers. Whatever your feelings about each other, you are all locked into a situation when, for the most of your waking day, you are involved in the same end product. Their job and motivation within that may be totally different from yours but the sheer persistence of that common denominator will inevitably create a group empathy which the introduction of an outside element will undermine – particularly if this also has the leverage of a spouse.

The psychological ecology can't cope with this. Your staff know just how far they can push you, but your spouse is an unknown quantity. They can guess, however, that if they upset him/her, your life is going to become very miserable indeed, and that the knock-on effect will be out of all proportion to its cause. This will depress them and ultimately make them nervous, to the detriment of all that you are trying to build.

Office Parties

Office parties will happen whatever your personal wishes, and as they are the most virulent form of self-expression for the various egos, attitudes and pent-up emotions of those who are on your payroll it behoves you to keep in touch with what is going to go on. They will have a party whether you like it or not and things will happen which will, for a while, disturb the status quo. It is the one time in the year when everyone will be equal in the general way of things and their memory of that night, however blurred, will be with those that you rely upon for a very long time – often for ever.

There are two things that you must keep in mind. The first is that your spouse is absolutely no part of this and must *not* be there. The second is that this is not your party. You must keep sober, as however much Miss Letchingham is attached to your flybuttons, any involuntary movement on your part will be relayed round the ground within seconds and the thin red line between you and total anarchy will be well breached.

The occasion really is only a chance for Mr Honeywell in Accounts to talk on social terms to Miss Olivetti in the typing pool, and this is very commendable. Practically speaking, you cannot expect those who have been working under the very false constraints of a business life, which throws them together haphazardly into a framework which prohibits the normal process of human intercourse, not to have certain feelings and desires. They are not strangers, but they have been meeting across a crowded room for the last twelve months and, at the very least, they are curious. As this is the difference between man and monkeys there is nothing that you can or should do to stop it. As soon as Mr Ligotti from Admin. starts chatting up that spikey haired lad who you think drives a van, you should make your farewells and leave, and everyone will thank you for it. They will have enough trouble in the morning without having to worry what you might think.

What I have been talking about is the sort of semi-spontaneous party that somehow develops, almost without your knowledge, somewhere in the depths of your business, and is held either on the premises or at some place close to hand. As long as the party is a genuine expression of the wishes of all those involved, it can only be a good thing. You chip in an amount of cash for the general goodwill, and as long as they don't burn down the building you have done your part and everyone will feel the better for it, but as you become bigger or more conceited or both, your spouses or those of your associates will wish to take a part. Oh dear! What shambles I have seen when this fundamental expression of drink and lust is placed on a formal plane.

Firstly, this is or should be a party given by the workers, for the workers. The fact that you have given a fair percentage of the drinks needed does not detract from that. Quite the opposite – you have merely shown that you have acknowledged their importance to you and your business and your ties to them, and as long as you have not clasped or had clasped anything more than the right piece of flesh in the spirit of friendship and have not fallen over on the way out, you are a hero – which is great.

You try to convert this bacchanalian ritual to anything more than it is. You transfer it to what you, if you still cling to the thin threads of your previous civilization, would call a 'proper party'. You try and hold it in a 'proper place' and make it into the sort of event that reflects well upon you and your standing with your family and friends and you are going to wind up as many a pompous idiot that I have witnessed – mortified. Everyone has to go home and dress up, collect the spouse and come back. They all have to drive so no one can drink, and worst of all they cannot have even the illusion of lust.

My first office party was a marvel for me. I met the girl who I had fancied all year. We went off together, and had a very nice time indeed, so did everyone else. Next year the company had grown and moved and we had a formal occasion in rooms in Tottenham Court Road. Everybody was either pissed or pissed off and the Chairman of the whole concern, who last year heard 'Jolly Good Fellow' several times, was hit with bread rolls in the first thirty seconds of his spiritual message.

Most of our own staff parties were of the spontaneous piss-up variety. We once made the mistake of giving a 'special'. At the time we were on the edge of a big expansion. We had been experiencing much trade union pressure from within, which we thought we had resolved, and we mistakenly gave a party to celebrate the event. It was an open house and anyone could bring their boyfriend, girlfriend etc.

We had misjudged the short-term effects of the occasion. All the staff were there, but not their mates. We had a massive spread of food, drink and loud music, and they sat like vultures, eating and drinking everything in total silence. The party spirit was conspicuously absent. The odd one stood on a table and did a little dance, then one bit the ear of a security guard quite hard, and he, being a family man, left for hospital. That broke the ice, and for a while they did what they thought should be their own thing. There were about 200 youngish girls there, all selected for their strength of mind and physical attributes and, however polite you might wish to be about it, they wrecked the joint. The union area manager, for whom I already had some sympathy, arrived as the going was getting on the heavy side, and I watched him walk among his members. He was a good and diligent man, and I could see that he was getting a bit out of his depth. So I waded through this heaving mass of, let me not demean them in the least bit, incredibly beautiful girls, and took him to my office, where I gave him a drink and he brushed himself down. When he had got himself half together he asked 'Who are those birds?', to which I had to reply, 'Your members, brother'. We had another drink and I showed him down the back stairs, and never saw him again. But relations with the union were noticeably more relaxed at our next meeting, and improved quickly from then on.

Relations

Offspring and all kinds of in-laws should also be avoided, except in extreme circumstances. Their introduction into the business will act as a great depressant on the hopes and ambitions of the rest of the staff. However far down the ladder you start them off, you will not fool the others that they will not have preferential treatment, particularly in the case of sons and daughters. I once reported to a director whose father was chairman and founder of the business and whose brother was the M.D. I felt really sorry for him, as his whole life was dominated by the need to prove himself. He would point out how he had started in the Post Room and worked his way up slowly on his merits, but nobody liked to point out that you had to be some sort of genius to go from Post Boy to Director in two years, as it would probably have made him cry, so the task of the executives under him was made doubly hard by the need to support his ego. He was a very nice man, and nobody wanted to upset him. The father was well past it, and he and his brother made great efforts to attract the proper talent into the firm, but having got it there they had no idea what to do with it. Quite soon the whole thing started to disintegrate and finally closed, simply because the sons, who would have been perfectly alright chugging on as middle managers in a large concern, had neither the ability nor experience to cope when things started to go wrong. If you really want your children to take over from you, send them off to someone else's company where they can learn and make their mistakes in a truly competitive situation and, hopefully, make progress. If they are not good enough to make their way to the top on their own merits in another outfit then you are doing yourself no favour by having them messing around with yours. It will end in disaster.

Obviously, there are exceptions. The Hoovers and Fords, for example, have done very well indeed by perpetuating a dynasty, and there must be countless other success stories. The one I like most is that of the Mars Bar Company. Mr Mars in the USA sends his son off into the world with the European rights and little else. Some years later the son comes back, so successful that he takes over the father. Mr Mars must have been a happy man. These are the exceptions, however. The average entrepreneur coming to the end of his time is probably better off bringing in professional managers or selling out, or simply packing it in and going home, than he is handing over to children whose sole attribute is that they are of his blood, but it must be a hard decision to make.

You

However, wives and children, friends and relatives are nothing in comparison to the main problem that must be faced, and that is you. Although you are the biggest fish in the pond and those who work for you look up to you, if only as the provider of their daily bread, you are unlikely to be of a saintly disposition and the temptations and opportunities for you to make a fool of yourself are many. One thing is certain. If you do start to veer from the straight and narrow you are going to be spotted in the end, probably sooner rather than later, and the ramifications and problems this can cause can be out of all proportion to the original sin.

To say that everyone would like to sleep with the boss is rubbish, but your position does give you a certain inside track in these matters, and you must be extraordinarily careful that you do not use it. Although you are allowed the odd hiccup you are not expected to display the normal human weaknesses, particularly in the areas of drunkenness and lechery, nor, and you must watch this, are your managers. However cautious you and they may be, it's absolutely impossible to keep the little liaison or regular hitting of the bottle secret for very long, and your failure to do so will cause you to lose an enormous amount of face with your staff, and a corresponding amount of respect and goodwill. What is worse, if you are not careful, is that soon they will all be at it, particularly the drink, which can cause untold damage to your business.

Many larger companies have a director's dining room, which I think is a big mistake. When one goes to visit them, the first question is, 'Will you stay to lunch?', and you know that unless you can achieve the aim of your visit before then, the day is over and you might as well have stayed at home. Inevitably there is a waiter in attendance, who is mentally totting up the drinks consumed and reporting back to his mates and thus to the entire business. Who can blame them, the factory or office worker, whose job is probably miserable anyway, for having a few themselves? Many businesses are definitely at half-cock after lunch. People start stitching themselves into the garments they are making, the general accident rate goes up and at the end of the day they have a few more to perk themselves up. The next morning some of those don't feel like it that day and things can start to come unstuck on a grand scale. If you really need a drink that badly, go a long way away where there are no witnesses and hope no one notices you on your return, but over a period they are bound to and the rot will set in.

Matters of the heart are an altogether more dangerous game. Victorian books are full of cautionary tales of mill girls being brought to ruin by their unscrupulous employers. There aren't too many tales of mill boys meeting their downfall at the hands of wicked female mill owners, though, and I must confess that in my youth I was, much to my chagrin, subjected to very little physical abuse from ladies who were my commercial superiors, so at the risk of drawing sexual distinctions I should point out that this is mainly a male problem. Although you always find randy idiots of all sexes and all ages, somehow, amongst the young, these things managed to be reduced to a natural perspective, and it is not until you and your managers reach an age when they should perhaps 'know better' that true problems arise.

The male menopause is a marvellous thing to behold. It usually occurs between the ages of 40 and 50 and is associated with a sudden change of circumstances for the better. Your man thinks that he has 'suddenly made it' and as he now has many of the status symbols that he did not possess at the age of 20 – money, position, fast cars for example – he mentally regresses to that era, and starts to act accordingly. Unfortunately, the only younger people he knows, apart from friends of his children, are working in his business, or worse, if he is a senior and trusted executive, in your business.

I once had to observe at close quarters the embarrassing situations this produces. For openers, I had to go to lunch with one of my investors, and some young lady who had attracted his fancy. I sat there, half listening while the lady's merits were flogged to me, and by the time the cheese arrived I could see that I would have to offer her a job, which was obviously what the whole charade was about, and which she demurely accepted. I made my excuses and left – I was obviously not part of the plan for the afternoon.

Apart from a propensity to wear see-through blouses, the girl was perfectly pleasant. I invented a job where she could not do much harm, and thought nothing more of it. Not so my management team who, being much faster than I was in seeing the advantages of a double agent, started feeding her with some real gems, guaranteed to drive our investor up the wall. He would call me in the middle of the night demanding to know if I was aware that this, that, and the other was going on. Eventually I called the managers together and explained that although what they were doing was highly amusing, I was the one getting the thin end of it so I wanted to be in on the joke, and that such a conduit for the dissemination of false information had to be looked after and nurtured for times of need. However, the temptation to make mischief was too much for everyone, and we would feed in some particularly spicy material, to see how long it took to get back.

I went to meet the man one morning and, arriving early, found him canoodling with another, and sure enough the girl of the transparent tops left our employment just after, and that was that. This new liaison created some fairly serious problems. The lady, who was elevated to Personal Assistant with a desk outside her lover's office, lived in a block of flats in the small town where his company was located. Several other employees of the firm lived nearby. Our hero would come roaring up at night in his fancy red machine, and take his leave in the morning with plenty of revs and wheel spin. Inevitably a friend passed the good news on to his wife, and the next minute there are tears and confrontations all round and he winds up in church with the charmer in question.

He was so besotted with his new lady that he decided that she was just what *we* needed to support our image, and we had a running battle from that time on to keep her simpering little person out of our hair. The whole affair caused a monumental amount of animosity between ourselves and her husband, and probably was an important factor to the falling out which was contributory to the demise of our business – all because a menopausal man could not keep his trousers in place.

9

Exports

Here in Britain we have a strange attitude to the idea of selling our products in other countries. Horror stories abound of dishonest foreigners, ripping off innocent or ignorant Brits. The export manager, if you have one, is an unwelcome guest at the feast, the orders he produces fraught with dangers and difficulties. Visions of Letters of Credit ticking away like time bombs and an atmosphere of unease and anxiety appear at the sound of the word export.

Much of this concern is understandable. People and attitudes are different out there. Degrees of tolerance, behaviour patterns and business ethics vary enormously from country to country and if you sit back at home, taking the odd order and shipping products off into the blue, you are going to come adrift. Imagine what it must be like for a poor old foreigner trying to do business in the UK. It is tough enough for you in your own country, let alone for a stranger, and the same applies to you when you venture abroad.

However, if you do not make the effort you will be denying yourself the opportunity of addressing a market umpteen times larger than the British Isles, which is a very small place indeed. Who knows, your humble product, which is staggering along going nowhere, may be exactly the thing to tickle the fancy of the masses in places that you never heard of and if you do not get out there and see what is going on, you will never know what might have been.

Most creative people will tell you that Britain is one of the worst countries in the world for the appreciation of the designer's art. Many would maintain that the better the design the less it is wanted. In most other countries it is the reverse, so if your product or service is a bit special you may find that you have been beating your brains out here, whereas elsewhere your ideas will be appreciated and you can prosper.

You will have to start your market research all over again, country by country. The main question, the answers to which you must know before understanding your chances in any particular market place, is that of price and profit. It is no good assuming that, because shoes are very expensive in Germany, and those same items sitting on your warehouse floor are, in comparison, very cheap, you are going to make a killing, unless you know exactly how much it is going to cost you to sell your product, transport it to the back door of the customer, pay all the various duties and commissions on the way and allow the eventual outlet to take whatever profit is the norm. All these things can vary substantially from market to market, and even if you are not actually paying everything yourself, somebody is going to have to and the price will increase accordingly, or, in real terms, the amount that you have to play with at your end will decrease. All over the world, people work backwards. They do not care how much an item has cost you to produce, they know what it is worth to them and their customers, and therefore what price they will pay. The same with your sales people, distributors or whatever system you are using – they want their percentage to be slightly higher than they would expect from a local product, because of the additional aggravation factor that importing involves, and if there is nothing left for you, it is too bad.

Before you start on any really heavy expenditure make sure that commercially it is worthwhile. Even if you are making all the initial running yourself, with no sales commissions between you and your ultimate customer, make allowances in your price for this outgoing in the future. It is pointless opening up a market to discover that you cannot afford the costs of its exploitation.

Here are some of the factors that you must take into account, together with a few technical terms to get you on your way.

Freight and Duty There are four ways of sending bulk items across international boundaries, whether by air, sea, or road. These are –
(i)   Ex-factory: this is easiest for you. Your customer comes to your warehouse, collects the goods, and that is the last you see of them. Only very large customers importing big quantities will want to do this, and then only if they have their own set-up in your country. Most shipping agents can also arrange this service.

(ii) F.O.B. (Free on Board): This means just that. You deliver
      to their shippers and are responsible for all costs until it is
      on the actual ship, plane or lorry that is going to take the
      goods all-or part-way to their ultimate destination.

(iii) C.I.F. (Carriage, Insurance, Freight): Here you pay for
      everything until it actually lands in your customer's own
      country. I would try and avoid this, particularly if you are
      the recipient of a Letter of Credit. If, say, your customer is
      in Italy, and you have to deliver to the Italian airport by a
      certain date, and there is a strike in Milan, you cannot
      deliver, and the L/C is broken. There are all sorts of clauses
      about industrial action and Acts of God, but it becomes a
      messy business, and you will be at best kept waiting for
      your money for quite a while.

(iv) Free Domicile: You deliver to your customer's back door,
      paying everything, freight, duty, clearing agents fee, the
      works.

If you are to really penetrate a market, at some stage you will
have to use this last method if you are to deal with the vast bulk of
customers, who have no experience of importing, and who
merely want the merchandise to arrive as if they were buying
locally. This can involve you in some very awkward moments,
because so much depends on the activities of the local clearing
agent, who is normally an associate of your (UK) shipping agent.
I use the term associate in the loosest sense, as very often the
local firm has only a 'paper' relationship with your UK company,
who have never seen them in their life. The local clearing expert
has, in most countries, to pay all duties up front, which he does
not like. You will be bombarded by requests for money, backed
by threats of legal action or spot fines from the Customs
Department aimed either at you, or worse, your innocent
customer. So life can be very fraught.

Whichever method you employ, the total costs involved in the
movement of merchandise from you to the destination are about
the same, and someone has to incorporate them into the real cost
of your product, but it can make a very big difference to you
which method you employ in two crucial areas.

First, cash flow. If we take an extreme case where you are

selling an ornamented garment free domicile to a customer in Los Angeles, USA, by air freight. Duty is 33% and charges around 12%, so, on top of the cost of your product, you are going to pay out 45% of your invoice total well before your customer is going to pay you. This can easily be more than the cost of manufacturing the product in the first place, so the capital needed to finance this particular transaction is correspondingly higher. Also you had better be sure that the money is there when it is needed, or that particular consignment is going to be sitting in Customs at L.A.X. clocking up extortionate storage charges and penalties, and can even wind up being sold off at auction if you cannot afford to get it out.

Second, sales agents' commission and discounts. We will go into how you might organize your selling in a moment, but if you are using local agents they will want to be paid their percentage on the face value of the invoice, which means that you are paying out another, say, 15% on the 45% it has cost you to get the merchandise from A to B. Likewise, any quantity discounts you may enter into will all be based on the same gross figure and suddenly your margin can look very thin indeed. Make sure that you have taken absolutely everything into your calculations, done a worst position cash flow, and only go ahead if you are sure that you can both finance the operation over a long period, and that your real gross profit is worthwhile.

You have worked everything out, and there seems to be money in it, now what? You need contacts. If you have friends in the country involved, start there or visit or write to the local British Commercial Attaché – you might get lucky. Check out the Trade Fair situation, as these can be very productive and you can often get assistance from the Export Council. If you do show at a fair, however, be extremely cautious of the customers and would-be distributors that may approach you. The import/export world attracts a large number of people whose mouths and ambitions are much larger than their pockets, and you, sitting in your little stand, with the world passing you by without a glance, are in just the frame of mind to be suckered. Trade Fairs are full of buyers who cannot get credit from their own countrymen and would-be distributors who are without funds; of more import- ance to you than any orders they may be placing is their ability to pay, so it is essential that you get details of their bank account number and full company name which you can check out on your return to the UK. Trade Fairs are like angling. You can sit there all day and nothing happens, and then, suddenly, you have hooked the big one. You need to be an unshakeable optimist because it can be very depressing work.

Alternatively, you can make a direct approach to customers that you feel would be suitable, and add prestige to your product if you can name them as stockists at a later date. Ring, do not write. An overseas telephone call is much more impressive to a buyer than a letter and can get you an appointment, whereas your carefully penned sales pitch may go straight in the waste paper basket.

It is relatively simple to place your product with a department store. They have large areas to fill, and are always on the look out for new items, and as long as product and price are OK they will generally place some sort of an order, but that is usually as far as it goes. You will be treated as a novelty or promotion and will rarely see any further business, however excited everybody may be at the time. United States department stores are bad in this respect. They eat up newcomers, extract the juice and spit them out in five minutes.

If you are fortunate enough to score with a multiple group, then you are possibly in another league entirely. Chain stores are very hard to penetrate, but have much greater commitment to the notion of sales per foot and other yardsticks that encourage them to make a real effort to push your line. They will have a very good idea of their importance to you and the going price of your product. They will therefore do a very hard deal indeed, and although at the moment you have no salesmen's commission to pay and are probably selling F.O.B., you must keep the longer term in mind. In the future, should you wish to develop that market, you cannot have them selling at one price and everyone else at another that is much higher. You must make up your mind. Maybe the deal is so good, or your current need so great that you go for the short-term gain, and you may be right, but make sure that this is a conscious decision, not taken lightly.

Assuming that you have made this first beachhead into a new area, you must act quickly to expand while you have satisfied customers to trot out to other potential buyers. As we all know, things can go wrong, fast, and what you do not want are dissatisfied outlets knocking your stuff out at a 50% discount.

Obviously, you cannot monitor what is happening, sitting thousands of miles away. Although you may have done really good research in the initial stages, the situation both economically and competitively can change overnight, and suddenly the orders dry up and you have no idea why, until it is too late. To get anywhere you must have local representation, and you are back to the old argument, do you stay as a cottage industry, selling to a few select customers, perhaps using a Public Relations type person to generally keep things moving or do you go for the big time?

There is no pat answer. I know many big names in the design field who stayed exclusive and are, twenty years later, world-famous and wondering where the next meal is coming from. Others went for the big time and it did not work. You pays your money, and hope for the best. Practically, the less esoteric the product the more chance you have in the long haul. This applies anywhere, but particularly if you are addressing a world-wide audience.

Personally, I go for the volume, and hope for the best. This brings us back to the Distributor versus Agents question. As in the home market, the distributor is the easy way out, and if you can find the right one you can go like wild fire, but he can quickly cost you a vast amount of money. Sitting at a Trade Fair, feeling rejected, I did a deal with two nice people from Paris. Barbara and I went over, we did a great launch, and they opened up most of the big outlets and many smaller ones in about six weeks. The problem was that they simply did not have the money to finance the sales, and they went over their credit limit in about two weeks. 'Mais Fitz', they would whine, 'this is Au Printemps et Gallerie Lafayette, we must supply, or we lose the French market', and supply we did. In the end we could not afford to supply any more without payment, so we lost the market anyway and so much money that I do not want to think about it. Adieu Annie, and Christian, and Jollie Jacques. As far as the French stores are concerned, the poison has been placed that we do not deliver, which I suppose is perfectly true. If you don't try these things nothing will ever happen anyway, but they can be expensive.

My feeling about distributors is that, if you can find the right ones, i.e. those of financial substance, in the markets that you consider to be of minor importance in the long term, then they are your best bet. For those countries where your potential is great, forget them. You cannot afford to have others controlling a huge chunk of your income in a way that excludes your own active involvement. One day something better will come up for them and you will be out on your ear, wondering what hit you.

Agents, in a market that means much to you, are a different matter. You pay them on results and if one does not perform, you can sack him without damaging your whole distribution. You are therefore in charge of your own destiny just as much as you are in the UK. And if you esteem that market highly enough, and it starts to work, you should open your own small office there, or take in a local partner and make a serious effort. At the time of writing over 90% of my sales are exported and I know something of what I am talking about.

There is one major barrier in this business and that is documentation and local obstacles such as labelling and packaging. The general trend with most trading countries is to keep the amount of paperwork down, but the fact is that if your delivery is not accompanied by all the forms they want, properly completed, it will disappear, and will be both costly and difficult to extract. It also makes it late in arriving at its destination which is usually most damaging of all. If you aspire to exportation, it is essential, however boring it may appear at the time, that you, the Boss, knows every wrinkle and dimple of the document game, in every country to which you are shipping. Furthermore, there is much bribery and nodding and winking taking place at most points of entry and you must be sure that the people who are representing you are on the inside of this very closed circle.

Some years ago we were launching a product in Italy. We had a big party, all the heavies from the press and some potential customers coming to see us. The Sunday of the week we were set to go, our shipping agents, reputedly the world's largest, had a spread in the *Sunday Times* telling the world how they would not capitulate to the Mafia. I was hoping that our shipment had been released before this announcement reached the local gentry. We kept checking, but for our multinational agent this was a 'local problem' and there was nothing to be done. Our friends in Milan kept telling us to come out. We arrived, kisses, kisses, and someone says to me in Italian words that I can just understand, 'You have a problem and I am here to fix it'. I say 'How much?' and it is £25. Sitting in the street, revving his truck is a wide eyed boy, and off he goes like Ascari, and back he comes two hours later, unscathed, and we are in business. This brings me to the major difference between success and failure, which is attitude – yours and theirs. We are very happy to be British, they are delighted to be Americans, Nicaraguans, or even, as we have been conditioned not to think, even Russians. Each country with which you become involved believes that they and their way of life is the right one. There is no point in your going in there and thinking that you are walking on water. You are a foreigner and must adapt to their way or you will be rejected.

How do you do it? You leave the smaller markets to look after themselves, and the further away you are, physically, from them, the more you must cut down your visits, as that is where money can disappear. In the big markets, you should develop your ethnic acquaintances as fast as possible. If you do not have any, employ people as soon as you can afford it to keep the day-to-day running moving nicely, or as nicely as possible in your absence, and spend as much time there as it takes to establish yourself as a genuine competitor in the long term.

The biggest, but not the only place where you can really make the megabucks is the USA. This is clearly the richest market on earth, and if you export you are inevitably going to try your luck here. Millions of words have been written about North America and its inhabitants. All your life you have been bombarded by the media with tales of American history and day-to-day living. Being British you have probably fallen for the old 'over-paid, over-sexed and over here' story. Returning tourists have told you how much the American citizen respects us, how our accent is venerated and generally how ripe they are for the plucking. Returning businessmen will have another angle entirely, with stories of indecision, inefficiency, and probably duplicity.

The truth is that the American way of commerce is very

different from that of our own. Our problem is that, because of the similarity of language and our secondhand knowledge of American life, it takes much longer for this to sink in. If we are in an obviously foreign place, such as China, where the differences between us are entirely visible, we are on our guard immediately.

The average American is an extremely polite person, far more courteous than the average Briton. They will go a long way to make strangers feel at home, and they will enter into business discussions and examine deals much more readily than would a European, but this does not mean that they are any less astute – far from it. Because they are, as a race, more practised in the art of negotiation they are very good at it indeed, at every level. Don't forget, next time you are cursing the driver of a yellow cab, who has stuck you in a traffic jam on the way to the airport, and whose English is near unintelligible, that his medallion (or licence to operate) has a value (in New York anyway) of over $100,000. Flick mentally through your own assets, and you may start to realize what you are up against.

Most important of all, personal contact has more value in the USA than anywhere else I know. If you are to make a success, you must physically be there as much as you possibly can, and if not, use the telephone. Don't forget, America is full of Americans wheeling and dealing, all day long, and the moment you are gone your place is taken by a queue of others, pushing and shoving to replace you. This is true in any country, but nowhere more so than the States. To make any lasting impact you must either be there yourself, or quickly take on local partners or associates, or your effort will be losing momentum before you get on the aeroplane home. If you treat it properly, America can make your fortune, but take it for granted and you will end up as just another disgruntled entrepreneur, moaning that you were robbed.

10

Afterthoughts

So far I have tried to give you a broad view of the sort of situations in which you might find yourself, and the general attitude that you must take if you are going to make your way. Each area that I have covered is the subject of many deep and detailed publications, and you can make a life's work of educating yourself in the theory and application of the Commercial Art. You can attend courses in your local Poly and graduate right the way through Harvard Business School. (The only person I have met who attended that academy had made several millions in a very short time and was in the process of being investigated by the Fraud Squad – there must have been a gap in the curriculum, or maybe he missed a few classes.)

You must not allow your lack of knowledge to inhibit you when you start. You will find that you learn fast enough as problems crop up from day-to-day. If you don't, you won't survive five minutes, but all the learning on earth will not help you if your drive and determination are not concentrated on going forward – I know many extremely successful people who can hardly write, let alone add up. A few years ago I was discussing with a would-be genius a possible joint venture. I outlined my plans and he picked up a minor point and asked 'Isn't that against the Companies Act?'. I realized that after 20 years of being in business, I had never even heard of the Companies Act, and anyway, if that was all he could say, I wanted no part of him – end of association.

I am not proud of this ignorance. It is merely that I had never come across that Act and had no need to bother about it. If it ever does become a factor in my life, there will always be someone to ask. Take football; if you always worry about being offside, you will never get near the goal anyway. You just have to be broadly aware of legal right and wrong and take it from there. I am not advocating ignorance – the more you know the better prepared you will be and your decisions will have a sounder base – but the knowledge in itself is irrelevant. You have no time to become an

105

expert in anything but the one subject that must preoccupy you, *success*.

Here are a few parting thoughts that do not fall under any of the headings that I have covered but may come in handy.

Timing When dealing with others, both in and outside your own business, the effectiveness of what you do and how you do it is determined by *when* you do it. If you pick your time correctly you can achieve, or get away with, a vast amount more than you might ever have imagined, but pushing an idea or a demand at the very wrong moment means that it will bite the dust. In the middle there are times that are better or worse but that are still not very good. As this whole question is of great importance you should spend a fair proportion of your own waking hours in studying the problem.

You must understand that your own desire to communicate, either through enthusiasm or desperation, is irrelevant. You may well need a decision or a big order or contract tomorrow for very pressing reasons of your own. You may even want to reward employees who have just worked 48 hours without sleep on your behalf, but you cannot press an appointment with the buyer to do it, or you will lose the deal and your staff will be so exhausted that the impact of your appreciation and generosity will be forgotten by the next morning, if it ever sank in at all. Believe me, these are not extreme examples. I have been called at midnight by happy people who have a great idea. A salesman from a company that I had never heard of once forced himself into my office, furious that he had not received a repeat order for a couple of thousand pounds when I was sitting there white faced and worrying about how to pay a wage cheque of over £20,000 the next day.

Once when I was selling advertising space I was stupidly directed to take a lift to the upper floors of the H.Q. of a very big company. I walked right into a very grave meeting of City Gents who looked at me with considerable surprise. I was quick enough to see that something was amiss but too gauche to retire with honour. I blurted out that I was there to see Mr X and was politely directed back to reception. Next morning I read that the company had been taken over, I had been in amongst the directors at the last rites. That was bad timing. When I arrived at the right office I explained, again being young, what I had just done, and the advertising manager thanked me very much and showed me out – no sale. That was stupidity. A more experienced person would have realized that he was out of his league, and bolted to the nearest licensed premises.

Good timing is a combination or common sense, careful thought and luck. If you do not apply the first two ingredients you will rarely manage the third. There are a few fundamentals that I have come across and that you should consider. First, your own time scale, however pressing, is very different from that of the people to whom you are talking. You must therefore only address them when you think that they are ready – not because you happen to have the hots. This can mean a severe curtailing of your natural desire to get things done even with your closest associates. If you have partners or directors their natural and human reaction will be to want to solve the problem before they go home that night, or at least they will wish to think that it is over, so that they can return triumphant in their wisdom to the warmth of their nests.

You, being the leader, will have no such delusions. Your nest is only as warm as the last financial egg that you have laid, and while your colleagues depart happily to the club or pub you will be worrying not about what you have all agreed, but how you are going to be able to make it happen, and the key question will be 'when?' You must therefore study the circumstances and your own thought-patterns, to judge your reaction to a particular approach at a certain time, and then try to project your response to this same situation in the mind of your quarry. For quarry it is, be it a not-so-humble buyer, your entire staff or a person with large amounts of cash who is vaguely interested in your enterprise.

The rules are so obvious that I fear to mention them, but as they have been broken so many times both by myself going out and others coming in they are probably worth a thought:

(a) Do not try and force commitments on people who, however much power they may have, do not have the budget or authority to make the decision you want at the time that you need it. They will have to say no, whereas on another day their answer might have been yes. By hitting them at the wrong time you have in their own eyes demeaned them and they will not like you for it.

(b) Equally important, do not make a move until you are quite sure that you are ready in both preparation and attitude. You may have worked out exactly what you want to achieve from a meeting or conversation, but are you in the right frame of mind to make your point with maximum effect? Be sure that there is nothing else clouding your brain when the moment comes, particularly if it is of the 'big problem' variety. Your preoccupation will be reflected in your attitude and even in your voice, and you will be less than your best. I always try to avoid long-range appointments of a critical nature. Who knows what problems you are going to be facing two weeks from now and what your priorities and mental state will be?

(c) Monday mornings and Friday afternoons are bad times for the average executive simply because on the Friday their sole desire is to arrive happy at their time of rest, to enjoy fully the fruits of their labour. They then spend the entire weekend worrying about what is going to happen when they get back, and on Monday they have enough problems without you adding to them.

Patience is the key. You are the fisherman and you must be certain that your fish is as near to hooking itself as you are going to achieve before you strike, however frantic you are to have it in the net.

This is possibly the only occasion when I would suggest you should take a brief look backwards and glance at moves that you have made, good or bad and with the strength of hindsight, analyse the result. You will probably find that most of your big triumphs or disasters have had little to do with your basic premise, however correct. It was the moment that you went up front that was the decisive factor. If you get it right, everyone calls it luck, if it fails, you are called an idiot. The truth is somewhere between, but only you know where. Take nothing for granted, however. What you did yesterday, even if it has been done successfully everyday for the last two years, is only a vague pointer to what you should be doing tomorrow morning.

Risks You did not go into business for the quiet life, and if you are to make progress you will have to take chances – the trick is to minimize your exposure, the 'down side', as bankers like to say. Look upon yourself as a bookmaker (you may even be one) and seek to lay off the odds. Most successful people will be in that position because they avoided failure along the way. They did this because they had fall-back positions, however drastic, pre-planned and organized in their own minds for use in the event that their ideas did not work out. Alongside their enthusiasm they had the sense to know that they could not always be right.

Good Things You may be onto one of these and, God willing, it may last forever, but don't bank on it, because if you are, there will be thousands trying to pull you off. For example, one of the best situations for a UK manufacturing company is to be a supplier to Marks & Spencer, and undoubtedly many millions have been made this way, but you wait until the great Lord Marks opens its mouth and speaks when times are bad. Suddenly your margins are being cut, and if you are unhappy there is someone round the corner to take your place. For every successful company in the hands of one customer, there are hundreds who wish that they had never heard of them. The big outlets did not get there by messing about. They have their own interests to look after, and their shareholders, and their pensions, and you are right at the back of their concern. You know that, because your own margins are being pinched, and if someone walks in tomorrow with the same deal at a lower price you will take it – I hope.

Your Word The notion that anyone's word is their bond is long dead, if in fact it ever lived, but your words, as the Boss, must be taken as gospel. Unfortunately the truth changes in line with your circumstances. You may tell your employees that they will have a pay rise next month, but business goes bad and you cannot

109

afford it. You say, 'I will pay you next week', having just banked a large cheque, and it bounces. You give an extra week off at Christmas and you receive a large rush order that has to leave on January 5th. Suddenly you are a liar, you have broken your word and, however much you explain the circumstances, you have lost a degree of trust and reliability which you cannot afford. As the Boss you are expected to be all-seeing and -knowing, which is impossible. In the certain knowledge that you are going to be thought dishonest, or at best shifty, sometimes by someone, the best you can do is to minimize the risk. It is very easy to tell people what they want to hear and be a short-term hero, but you are very much better off saying no, until what you are about to commit yourself to is, at least, a racing certainty.

Decisions Leave your decisions as late as possible, at least until you have narrowed the odds, but when the moment comes you must make your mind up and stick to it. I was doing National Service when I was asked to referee a game of soccer between two very rugged squads. They were kicking the stuffing out of each other and enjoying the match and my part was easy until there was a disputed goal. It was very close and I had no idea as to the right decision. Instantly 22 heavies changed from mates to a lynching mob. One of the Captains was a particular friend. 'Make your poxy mind up you . . . ' he bellowed, and I did, sharpish, as we say. One side cursed, the other cheered and the game went on. There is a moment when any decisions are better than none, and you are the only one who can make them.

Loyalty A definition of commercial loyalty is that you look after those who do the same for you. At the most negative level no one is going to jump off a bridge to save your neck, neither must you for them. So do not expect too much of your partners, suppliers or staff if your situation changes. They are only loyal to you because of your standing, and if this alters or is reduced in any way you have a problem, and those who have gained the most from you will be the first to turn. Those who have been robbing you over the years will feel a certain pity for you and stay as close as ever, usually to make certain that there is no more blood left, but those who were weeping with pleasure and gratitude when

110

you elevated them will, in hard times, turn on you as the person who ruined their lives. They will sue you, blackmail you, denounce you to the newspapers, and will convince themselves beyond all reason that you are Public Enemy No. 1.

I say this with some feeling, because during our Biba phase, which was many years ago, we had what we thought was a fine cadre of dedicated executives around us, and so they were, until we happened to get well sandbagged and out of that particular line of activity. The good bit was that amongst all the dross and rabble emerged some people that one could honestly say came up as friends, and that was very nice to find. Please remember my experience and do not see yourself as anything but a meal ticket to 99% of those around you.

Do Unto Others As the Boss you will spend most of your life being nice to people who have you by the throat. You need them to survive. Some may be quite pleasant and others a nightmare but you have to get them to do what you want, so you nod and smile and generally chat them up. It is important that, when roles are reversed, you do not use your position of power to abuse those who need you. You should be one who is different. By this I do not mean you to be stupid, or put up with rubbish, just that you should bear in mind that somebody loves them and if you have to let them down, make it as light as you can. You should not be the one that goes for the last drop of blood. It is very easy to bully those in a lesser position than yourself. I am not saying be soft, merely considerate. Anyway, who knows where they might get to in the future. We sacked a shop girl for stealing once and she is now one of the most powerful Editors-in-Chief in the fashion world. Would we have taken the same action if we had known? I hope so, but I doubt it.

Megalomania Hitler had it and so can you, if you are not very careful. You, whatever level your business, have an extraordinary power over those around you. You make the decisions and your orders have to be obeyed. After the first few years as the Boss you may, if you survive, look back and think what an animal you were early on, and if your attitude has not changed after a while, perhaps you should think about it. Being human,

111

you will find yourself revelling in the power and status of your new position, acting a part and doing things to demonstrate, mainly to yourself, what a great person you are. Clearly, this is very dangerous. Instead of impressing all those around you with your brilliance and acumen, they probably have you down as a conceited little ***** and will be busy trying to rip you off before the ship sinks,or at least they can change boats.

It is very easy, if you have an immediate success, to become carried away with the notion of your own infallibility. When trouble starts, you blame everyone but yourself and wind up sitting in a mental bunker, giving orders to imaginary armies, which have long since deserted. I know dozens of ex-geniuses of my generation, who were driving Ferraris when I could hardly afford the bus, and who have spent the last twenty years wondering what happened. Do not be one of them.

What is the difference between those who make it and those who do not? I don't think there is any one answer, but Mr Kroc of McDonald's fame was probably not far off when he identified persistence as the main factor. If you are reading this, you are not dead yet. Perhaps you haven't started, or are on your own, fighting it out and wondering why you bothered. This is literally a battle to the death, and the last man standing wins the game. So whatever happens, keep going and you will get there. Once you stop you are lost. It is that simple and that hard.

Personally, I am a great believer in prayer.